Twist Your Fate

7 Steps to Fortune

Geof Gray-Cobb

Schiffer Publishing Ltd

4880 Lower Valley Road, Atglen, Pennsylvania 19310

Cover Photo *by Dinah Roseberry*

Background Photos:
ear © Candyman.
Image from BigStockPhoto.com.
Icy Stone Steps © Simon Grenfell.
Image from BigStockPhoto.com
White Satin #2 © Marilynv.
Image from BigStockPhoto.com

Designed by Stephanie Daugherty
Type set in ShellyAllegro BT/NewBskvll BT

ISBN: 978-0-7643-2962-3

Printed in China

Schiffer Books are available at special discounts for
bulk purchases for sales promotions or premiums.
Special editions, including personalized covers,
corporate imprints, and excerpts can be created
in large quantities for special needs. For more
information contact the publisher:

Published by Schiffer Publishing Ltd.
4880 Lower Valley Road
Atglen, PA 19310
Phone: (610) 593-1777; Fax: (610) 593-2002
E-mail: Info@schifferbooks.com

For the largest selection of fine reference books
on this and related subjects, please visit our web
site at **www.schifferbooks.com.** We are always
looking for people to write books on new and
related subjects. If you have an idea for a book
please contact us at the above address.

This book may be purchased from the publisher.
Include $5.00 for shipping. Please try your
bookstore first. You may write for a free catalog.

In Europe, Schiffer books are distributed by
Bushwood Books
6 Marksbury Ave.
Kew Gardens
Surrey TW9 4JF England
Phone: 44 (0) 20 8392-8585;
Fax: 44 (0) 20 8392-9876
E-mail: info@bushwoodbooks.co.uk
Website: www.bushwoodbooks.co.uk

Free postage in the U.K., Europe; air mail at cost.

Dedication

To my wife, Maiya, after more than a half-century of her support and care, I'd never have made it without her.

It's choice—not chance—that determines your destiny.

—Jean Nidetch

Acknowledgements

Grateful thanks to all who contributed to the preparation of this book, and especially to Dinah Roseberry, my superlative editor, and all the rest of the team who fought so hard to make it all happen.

It's a funny thing: The more I practice, the luckier I get.

—Arnold Palmer

Contents

Go confidently in the direction of your dreams!
Live the life you've imagined.
As you simplify your life,
the law of the universe will be simipler.

—Henry David Thoreau

Foreword

Congratulations! You're a person who is bold enough to identify with this text and come out the other side with a new understanding about yourself and your world. My special thanks to you, and if the words here help to make your life easier or more productive, then the whole exercise has been well worth all the care and attention which a team of dedicated people put into creating this book. Thanks to everyone concerned: I'd never have made it without you.

This is a transcription of a portion of a session channeled from a life-force entity which calls itself Henry ('Arry) Plater, born in England and left this life around 1954.

"What I'm explaining to you is a system of personal transformation, and as I've said before (and probably will again), I've kept the theory and abstract content behind these instructions to a bare minimum, merely sufficient to describe what you should attempt to do for yourself.

"The approach that I'm going to show you here suggests that there are ways and means of connecting with a metaphysical energy which is greater than any physical force that you can bring to bear, and by tapping that energy you can transform your environment in the broadest sense of the word.

"I recommend you should master this book in easy steps. You'll get much greater effects if you read and fully understand and apply each section before reading the next one. I offer this work to you with the knowledge that its best results will occur when you regularly use the described techniques and thinking patterns, when you will then develop your inner talents to shape your own environment as much as your present stage of soul evolution can handle.

"May you find within these words meaning, application, and successful results. Those results depend purely on your motives and motivation, and in concluding this introduction, I would repeat: Use whatever part of this text you prefer in whatever order you wish. There is little padding within this text; each and every word, phrase and sentence has been included for a reason. Each exercise has a purpose, even if it's challenging to identify within the material, physical and logical universe that you are inhabiting at this time.

"I wish you peace and harmony during your quest."

—'Arry Plater

Introduction

Sharpen the Sword of Lady Luck

Fortunes come tumbling into some men's laps.

— Francis Bacon
Advancement of Learning

C arl Gustav Jung called it synchronicity.

He suggested that there is a relationship between a person's psychological state and the events which are somehow attracted to him or her. Or try it this way: some people are consistently luckier than others. Taking a step further, some people can personally influence these apparent random events so they can gain or manifest benefits. This book shows you how coincidences, chance, and luck can make synchronicity your master.

Reflecting on Dr. Jung's words, a while ago I was wondering how some people are winners and others are losers. Maybe it's a matter of sheer luck, and while chatting with my neighbor across the street, he said, "Do me a favor—if I didn't have bad luck, I wouldn't get no luck at all."

Now if that's you in a nutshell, hang tough. Here comes the cavalry with bugles blowing and flags waving. And you can blow your own trumpet and wave banners yourself, soon as you get into your good luck gear. Pin your ears back and listen just one cotton-pickin' minute. This book tests the idea that good fortune is an influence which can be recognized, and by applying clear-cut actions to your life you can sharpen the sword of Lady Luck so you acquire a larger slice of any good fortune that's going.

But first a question, even if it has broken your train of thought. How did you come across this book?

Chances are you may have bought it or received it as a gift from a friend. You might have heard about it, or had a couple of pages of it read to you by someone. Perhaps you picked it up while you were browsing in your local library. Possibly you clicked "Find" on your computer keyboard while you were looking for something else entirely, and even as you were doing a "Google" search, some of the words or the subject flashed up on your monitor and caught your attention.

Chances, Flukes, and Twists of Fate

For instance, one way or another you found this book. Certainly, a whole host of related events occurred before you finally saw this text in front of you. If a whole bunch of chances, flukes, and destiny patterns had occurred some *other* way earlier, you may never have seen nor read the words you're reading at this moment.

You might think about what could have happened if your friend had decided to gift you something else: Instead of this book, you may have been the happy recipient of a new CD. Another happenstance might have been that you decided to stay away from the library on the day you picked up this book, so some other reader took the book out and you missed it the next time you went browsing. And considering only one other possible hurdle, the whole shipment of books could have been sent to Brazil owing to some mislabeling error. The point is that there are a multitude of events that could have kept you totally unaware of the fact that this book, or these methods, exists.

Anything Can Happen, and Often Does!

You get the picture—it seems anything can happen, and often does, but in this case the *right* event happened: You got your hands on this book!

See where I am heading with this thought? I'm suggesting that there are some things that have taken place in your life which actually happened, while there are other events which, because you chose to make a different decision, were only possible events that *could have* happened, but actually failed to come about—at least in this space and time.

Now, if you're a total believer in fatalism which says that every event is predetermined by destiny and is inevitable, so what's going to happen will happen no matter what, we may be running on different philosophical tracks. Certainly, yours is an important personal concept, but in this particular case it may be marginal to the idea I'm proposing. Bear with me while I explain further.

What Happens Next in Your Life

I'm a personal believer in freewill, and my idea of what is in your future suggests that those decisions and actions that you take right now decide what happens next in your life. But whether you're a fatalist, a freewill proponent, or whether you go along with some other philosophy, you can easily follow the thinking of this book.

Peaks of Personal Accomplishment

As you read the various chapters that follow, you'll find the common thread of meaning: By picking up clues in your daily life, you can arrive at continual peaks of personal accomplishment which come from the use of the procedures I've clearly outlined.

Within this narrative are suggestions on how you can recognize chances, coincidences, and techniques that will, if you wish, enhance fundamental luck energies which are ready to help you, even if you're a bitter skeptic who's tried this kind of game before without any results.

A Specific Adaptation

Listen Up!
Try it this way: these procedures are simply a specific adaptation of Carl Jung's theory of synchronicity, and in Chapter 8, we'll discuss that distinction further. The Funk and Wagnalls dictionary definition of that 64-dollar five-syllable word says that "synchronicity is the temporal coincidence of two or more events linked together by meaning but without any causal connection."

Were you ready for that? What Jung means (I think) is that sometimes two events or incidents can happen at the same time, even though they're apparently logically unrelated, yet the combination of those two events produces a useful outcome.

For example, while I was writing an early chapter of this book, I heard about a lecture that was going to be delivered in Edmonton, Canada. The subject, life after death, interested me, but I knew I'd be unlikely to be able to attend the meeting. I was about 1,000 kilometers away at the time, so I telephoned my daughter, Viki, who lived on the outskirts of Edmonton, and suggested she might be interested in being present at the lecture.

After the presentation she and I made contact again and I asked her if the talk had been interesting and worthwhile. She agreed that the lecture contained thought-provoking concepts, but added, "Something I couldn't figure out, though. I had some questions for the researcher and when he'd answered some of my queries he suddenly said, 'Who's Walter?'"

"I didn't know anybody of that name," she said, "and neither did anyone in the hall. At least, nobody put their hand up and said anything. Yet the lecturer insisted that there was someone named Walter close by. He said the Walter person was already 'in spirit'—like deceased—and he had a message, not for me, but for my father."

The message from 'Walter' for me announced that he was fine (presumably in heaven) and "you should carry on with your project because it's going to bring an outstanding response."

The project? This book.

Now here's this odd incident: while we were chatting, Viki also asked if I myself knew anybody called Walter. I cudgeled my aging memory and opined I'd never known anyone of that name, so far as I recalled.

Was I ever wrong! Within an hour, my wife reminded me of two Walters I'd forgotten. One of them, a photographer and movie producer from Johannesburg, South Africa, was named Walter Verwey. We'd worked together for several years, until Walt went back to his native Holland around 1964 and we lost touch.

Then I found another reference to Walter, and this was even more compelling. A few days earlier, I'd been re-writing a piece of this book. I was dissatisfied with a description I'd written, and I was sorting through my notes, so I could replace a section about remarkable coincidences. Surprisingly, what should pop up in my mind but a reference I'd noted some time ago about a researcher and author named Dr. Grey Walter.

It was many years earlier I'd read Dr. Walter's book, *The Living Brain*, but his words were exactly the catalyst I needed to flesh out that particular part of my own narrative—you'll notice the reference in Chapter 7.

So, was it meaningful coincidence? I'll say it was, and I guess it's really unimportant whether Dr. Walter signed on to the Akashic Record to remind me that his book would be useful to me, or whether the Edmonton lecturer read my mind at a distance even before I'd remembered Dr. Walter's book and theories. I speculate we'll never fully appreciate what can happen in the human brain, but it's certainly odd that the lecturer should have picked up on the name of Walter.

Of course, being an intuitive person, he could have picked up the name from my mind, someone else's mind, or even from the knowledge I have in my memory that my birthday is the same as novelist Walter Scott who was known as the *Wizard of the North*. So many possibilities, and we can never comprehend such things totally, which is one of the fascinations of the application of this account.

Whether you call it synchronicity or just a twist of chance you might consider that *the Walter concept* came on stream for me at precisely the right moment.

And stop the presses, so I can tell you two further events which are truly synchronistic material. One is pure synchronicity which Jung states is "a glimpse into the underlying patterns of the universe."

I was surfing our local library, browsing some of the more offbeat books, and our indefatigable librarian (thanks Joanne; you're a marvel) who cheerfully unearths obscure books for my partner and I, said, "This one might be up your street, Geof, it looks weird enough." The book was about the spiritualist movement and I found it interesting enough but then on page 193 I really sat up and took notice.

Synchronicity again: Mina Crandon was a Boston medium (later, in this New Age, she'd be known as a channeler) and on Mina's first session she made contact with her brother. Alas, he'd been dead at least twelve years, but his blithe spirit told Mina that she had great clairvoyant gifts.

Sure enough, Mina soon developed a remarkable assortment of psychic skills. The spirits moved her in a whole host of ways, shoving objects around and even destroying some furniture. Melodious noises came out of nowhere, soft fragrances drifted by, and phantom lights blinked off and on. And who was the perpetrator of this mystical mayhem? None other, alleged Mina, than her dead brother, who happened to be called (wait for it) Walter.

The second fascinating event is in virtually the here-and-now. Maiya (my wife) and I started to embark on a major life-style change. In our province of Alberta, Canada, we decided to sell our acreage outside Edmonton with our 3,000 square foot home surrounded by woods and lawns. Our idea was to buy another property with less acreage, closer to town.

How about the *best laid plans* and all that neat stuff? Our property in Edmonton took only four days to sell and rather than rush around to buy another home, with winter setting in, we rented a small apartment until the following spring. Spring came and with it came a property boom. Suddenly stuff in even the $60,000 to $70,000 range started to move up in price, and soon, just very ordinary houses in suburbia were selling in the $200,000 and up mark. As far as the bank manager went, she said okay for that kind of a loan, but who needed a quarter-million dollar mortgage hanging on our necks for about twenty years? Neither of us are spring chickens, so we started looking for other possibilities.

Purely by chance, I was browsing the Internet when I noticed the next province along, Saskatchewan, had some remarkable bargains in real estate. We went online again and picked out seven houses which looked appealing, and we toured around, looking hopefully for our dream home... and, glory be, we found it. Our latest residence is a hundred years old, with all the amenities we need in a small Canadian town. The house has a sizeable yard, several cheerful ghosts, and enough rooms for my partner and I to write, sleep, eat, exercise, listen to music, and watch TV without tripping over each other. And the price was very right (I'll say it was—how about no mortgage at all?). Naturally, our *old lady* needed work in the way of heating, wiring, and new windows, and the plumbing was somewhat unpredictable but, as I wrote to a friend a while ago: "We fixed all that in a few months and we both find our house enchanting in the true magical sense of the word."

Mike and Daniel, our hard-working electricians, created miracles in the way of wiring, lighting, and power, but one person who deserves an even greater vote of thanks is a contractor who lives down that road a-piece. He made a fabulous job of fixing our home before the winter set in. Guess what his name is? Once again, synchronicity rules: his name is *Walter!*

Something Prompted You to Pick Up This Book

But before I get off track again, let's look at what occurred when you first found this book: Something happened to prompt you to pick it up. It's likely that your first sight of it was in the motivational section of your library or bookstore. On the other hand, you may have received it as a gift, as I mentioned before.

Perhaps at this very moment you're scan-reading to find out what it's about. So listen. This is a *How-To* guide. It shows you how to make changes in your life by using your own vital energies. Which may be an old concept to you, so your next question probably is: "What's in here that other motivational or inspirational books lack?"

Answer: "A set of ideas that will totally improve your everyday life."

Really? Yes, really! Read on. Now, your days will never be quite the same again, so be prepared. They will develop—in whatever areas you desire.

Chapter 1

The Secret to Happiness, Health, and Wealth.

A book should teach us to enjoy life ...

—Samuel Johnson
attributed

You've read or scan-read the introduction to this book. If you want to explore further into this enigmatic world of awareness, you should know that by absorbing the words here you'll be tweaking areas of your brain that may have remained slumbering for your whole life so far. And those areas contain energy reserves that can literally make you over into a new person.

Sure, you've heard claims like that before: Way back before the millennium, a rough count of motivational and awareness-altering methods in North America came up with a total of about 8,000 techniques—and new ones are being evolved every day. So in the here-and-now there are hundreds of books, seminars, workshops, cassettes, videos, CDs, classes, groups, even correspondence courses that promise you can improve your life by applying methods and techniques described or invented by their authors. Surely everything that can have been said has been said already?

You've Got It Made? In Your Dreams...

I mean, everywhere you look you run into ads telling you how to be successful. *Make Money the Easy Way, How to Survive The Depression, Money at No Interest, Make a Fortune from Real Estate* ... The list goes on. So surely we should all, like *Steinbeck*'s Lennie Small, be living on the *fatta de land*, when allegedly all you have to do is swipe your plastic and you've got it made?

Knowing How To Do It is Simple

That would be marvelous, right? Yet doing that kind of thing is no big deal. Leastwise, knowing how to do it is simple. Piece of cake. The *how* of it's been known and published for centuries. But knowing how, and regularly getting results, happens to be about two light years apart. So now it's time to turn your thinking into doing. It's time for something new—because this method does what it says: It shows you how to blend random chance into your regular life so that what you want to happen *does* happen, frequently in amazing ways. It may just seem like luck when your most marvelous fantasy is fulfilled, but you'll realize before long that you'll be able to woo Dame Fortune whenever you wish. And just playing the numbers or spinning the roulette wheel is only a tiny part of the story. This saga is a whole lot more constructive than that.

Results Will Appear For Your Personal Delight

What exactly can you do when you've got the method working well? The sky's the limit. Literally. Set up your journey of your awareness routine, work at it a little (did I promise you a full-blown rose garden?), and your results will appear in this world for your personal delight—and probably your private amazement.

I Had Trouble Believing It, Too.

Yes, I said *amazement* because a while back I was still in doubt about the marvels of synchronicity. I've discovered that whenever I apply the guidelines in this text, cool things keep happening, and I've learned to accept those benefits with appreciation.

The Final Secret?

Yet perhaps you've already tried umpteen techniques and found they were less efficient than you'd expected. So maybe you think there's another book which really, really has the final secret for making your wishes come true. Perhaps this book is the one.

Two ways you can go; three ways if one of those ways is to say, "The heck with it. This is all foolishness. I can do better things with my time than try to change my life by reading a book." That's fine. Your choice, naturally. But a second way to go is to continue to browse the motivational field. Read all the books you wish. Try the seminars. Attend the workshops. Invest in the videos, cassettes, and CDs. Join the groups and classes. Wait for the mail carrier to rush your *first exciting lesson* to be followed about twice a month by new and even more exciting lessons which cost you only two arms and a leg, and you can quit anytime guarantees.

Yes, you can do all that. Good luck in your search, and may you find exactly what you need and want. But...

See If This Method Is For You

The third thing you can do is to read this book and see if you're in tune with this approach.

Initially and many moons ago, I went down the metaphysical paths I mentioned earlier and found both frustration and achievement.

In the freewheeling sixties and seventies, I was also checking out the motivational action, and I went exploring in England, Iran, South Africa, the U.S., and Canada on the same sort of mystical quest and learned a lot of interesting stuff.

I'd already tried Emile Coué who, in about 1887, advised the reader to recite an affirmation attesting something like: "Every day and in every way I am getting better and better." Many people tried it and many found that it worked. And from that seed has grown the mighty motivational tree of which this book is a leaf.

Norman Vincent Peale, born in 1898, became virtual king of positive thinking techniques as he laid claim to a whole section of motivational turf. Napoleon Hill's inspirational books still grace the shelves. Catherine Ponder established a thoroughly valid offshoot with her *Open Your Mind to Prosperity*. Maxwell Maltz added further techniques in his *Psycho-Cybernetics*. Then in 1959, David J. Schwartz wrote *'The Magic of Thinking Big'* and in 1994, Eric Jensen wrote *'The Little Book of Big Motivation.'* And these are only a few examples of motivational works.

Meanwhile, I wrote a bunch of self-help books myself. My own first attempt, *The Miracle of New Avatar Power,* published in 1974 in New York, sold about 120,000 copies in hard-cover. I also wrote *Amazing Secrets of New Avatar Power* in 1978, *Secrets from Beyond the Pyramids*, 1979, and *Helping Yourself with Acupineology* in 1980. Even today, thirty years or more after those books were published, people come up to me at trade fairs or through e-mail and tell me they're still using those techniques; they say the old methods I wrote about are still playing useful roles in their lives—even in this new millennium.

The New Age Field Was Worth Exploring

When I first got started writing motivational material, the New Age field seemed to be worthwhile exploring. Even though it was the Age of Aquarius, many people considered the motivational arts and disciplines to be well inside the lunatic fringe of knowledge and experience. Strictly bughouse, said the scientific establishment: in brief, the claims of New Age practitioners were given a ripe *har-de-har* by most orthodox thinkers.

Who could blame the scoffing scientists? Even before the Fox sisters from Hydesville in Wayne County, New York, started their supernatural rap scene in 1848, the metaphysical field had sprouted a weedy harvest of charlatans and fakes, so any crops gleaned from there tended to be tainted with snake oil roots and similar carnival scams.

A Complex Maze of Illogical Evidence

So my early psychic treks took me deep into a complex maze of doubts, fakery, questionable data, and illogical evidence. Sometimes I wondered if I'd ever reach any kind of mother lode in the barren depths of that dubious labyrinth. Luckily, before I abandoned the search altogether, I found genuine nuggets of apparent truth, although most of them were sadly tarnished by the pollution of sensationalism and misconceptions that mask the real picture of the spiritual arts.

Mining those slabs of metaphysical rock and polishing them by experiment and selection brought surprises.

Without even a whiff of sulfur or a single devilish chuckle from demons, some techniques worked in this everyday world, producing what mystics have always said their powers were for: to bring harmony, happiness and peace to the individual. And, mark you, there's nothing especially mystical about this book and its contents. On the contrary, it's about as down-to-earth as your average vehicle owner's manual—and roughly twice as easy to understand. Sure, my earlier books have a solid thread of mystical energy application running through them, and this one, although different in concept, still maintains the thought that there are hidden energies that can work wonders for you, once you know how to use them.

A Greater Influence Than Many People Realize

The basic claim of my earlier works was that our minds have a much greater influence over our lives and surroundings than many people realize or will admit. Correctly applied, techniques that have been around since the pyramids were young can change negative to affirmative, depression to elation, and loser to winner.

Since these books of mine hit the shelves, scientists involved in quantum physics, atomic science, and medical research have been moving on their careful step-by-proven-step ways. To their apparent amazement, they have found themselves on collision courses with some of the claims and perceptions of the spiritual and mystical arts.

Backwards in Time

For instance, look at the phenomenon of particles of energy doing strange things like traveling backwards in time. Science is now prepared to consider that, and even more remarkable, behavior: John Gribbin wrote about such astounding activities in 1984 in his fascinating book on quantum physics, *In Search of Schrödinger's Cat.*

On a different wavelength, but definitely heading in related directions, author John William Dunne wrote *An Experiment With Time* as long ago as 1927. And somewhere in between, a mystical writer, Colin Bennett, wrote his meditational text, *Practical Time Travel.* Similar themes throughout, and now they're less improbable as they seemed to be decades ago.

More? Consider the way atoms defy being measured or located precisely. Their tiny eddies of energy—held together by forces that leveled Hiroshima—refuse to be pinned down to both a time and a place. Only one or the other. And that's most unscientific and illogical, yet it strikes an interesting resonance with the mystic's claim that time and space are an illusion of the mind.

Ancient Mystical Lore

The deeper science delves, the more some of its conclusions resemble ancient mystical lore. Current academic hypotheses are surmising that the universe as we know it may be a single network of intersecting energies, all mutually dependent on each other. Heading, inevitably, toward the thinking of the avatar on some frozen Tibetan peak who seeks total union with the Oneness that is All.

In a splendid echo of New Age views, doctors are heeding the theory that the human body and mind are incapable of being separated: what goes on in your brain may well have a provable effect on your physical well-being. And that moves the New Age adage: "You are as you think you are," from the airy field of philosophy into the day-to-day material world.

Rather like the science-fiction writers' ideas that have been overtaken by time to become actuality, many mystic perceptions are being caught up in the cogs of established thought and are proving to fit neatly into the machinery of this mundane world.

And along with those changing ideas, so I've changed my concepts of how to use personal energies to become prosperous, harmonious and successful.

Nothing On Some of My Early Suggestions...

Reading some of my earliest works, I find them downright naïve. Cracking a walnut with a steam-hammer has nothing on some of my early suggestions. For instance, I have trouble believing I once invited my readers to tap the powers of the four Archangels to help produce small sums of hard cash. But I did. It's in cold print. Reading some of my earliest works, I find that my thinking has changed over time and practice. For instance, I once invited my readers to tap the powers of the four Archangels to help produce small sums of hard cash. But now I realize that it is not necessary to gather one's angels.

So now, this book. Same theme: you can use your mind in specific ways to gain whatever you wish. And no way does this narrative deny the existence of Archangels, spiritual beings, or other mighty and superior forces of nature. On the contrary, I gladly accept the idea of such energies. What we have here is an updated, streamlined version of tapping into energies. To my delight (because I dislike bothering important entities with trivialities), I find it unnecessary to invoke Unseen Planes' energy to make personal life changes—although even that thought is open to interpretation.

Invocations and Affirmations

Yes, you'll find types of invocations and affirmations here, and they are indeed addressed to the Unseen—but to unseen levels of your own mind. And this being a practical book with minimal theory, I forbear to inquire what parts of your mind, brain, or soul play vital roles in the process of hitting your life targets. I neither know, nor do I especially care about that: Changing your life is the stated objective of this book and the true *how* of it I leave to theorists and philosophers.

Use This Book Like A Manual

Treat this book like any other instructional manual. You can learn to drive a car without knowing a thing about what goes on under the hood. Turn the key, push the right pedal, click this lever, and away you go.

That's how this book works: Follow the straightforward instructions and cosmic wheels will turn; then *bingo!* you're ready to discover whatever you desire. Health, wealth, emotional security, love, spiritual evolution—your choice entirely. Enjoy.

Prove me Right or Wrong

Now, so far that's just another unproven claim I'm making. You can prove me right or wrong by moving on through this book, trying the undemanding exercises and techniques, and then seeing the remarkable results. I invite you to turn the page and move on to the second chapter of this personal voyage of discovery.

Step 1:

Believe you can do it (because you can!).

Chapter 2

How to Get Rid of Misfortune for All Time

Experience has taught me this,
that we undo ourselves by impatience.

— Geof Gray-Cobb

B e comfortable. If you itch, scratch it. You want to cough? So cough. If you want to sneeze, then sneeze. And if you want to visit the rest room, go ahead.

In the Introduction I mentioned unhappy folks ironically saying: "If I didn't have bad luck, I wouldn't have any luck at all." Yes, there are many people like that, but you're excluded—as a person who's ready to make things happen the way you want them to, it's unlikely you'll be one of the gloomy people referred to previously.

But what if, through no fault of your own, you're one of those people who believe that calamity is just around the next corner? If that happens to be your attitude to life in general, now's the time to *keep* the idea of luck, but abandon the idea of *bad* luck, because what we're putting together here is a way to get rid of misfortune. And to get rid of it for all time—although if you're truly a hard-luck case, you'll maybe need a couple of kicks at this particular can before everything around you comes out confident and cheerful. But here's one of the hidden secrets...

Listen Up!
All you need to do to achieve that apparent lucky break is to think about it. Just that. Nothing more.

Some Conditions Apply, But They're Optional...

You're skeptical, and rightly so. What do the ad merchants say, usually in tiny print? "Some conditions apply." Yes, I guess a few conditions may apply, but they're more like suggestions rather than absolutely mandatory conditions. For instance, you probably realize it's pretty fruitless if you consistently tell yourself "It can't work" or you constantly think about similar negative points of view. Although such words and a negative mind-set will never actually negate the effects of synchronicity, they, by their specific type of energy, can put a temporary brake on progress.

So here's another scheme: Jump on the synchronicity ship. It's built to bring you to the safe harbor you've always hankered for and it will certainly help things along if you can use positive thoughts.

But even that's unnecessary. You can, if that's your psychological set, send wave after wave of dismal thoughts out into the ether, and coincidence will enthusiastically roll along in the right direction for you to be comfortable.

Twitches the Reins of Fate

You see, this approach works in a different way from simple positive thinking. What synchronicity does is to twitch the reins of fate or destiny so that somehow, somewhere, your dreams come true. Possibly, you may be able to actually see some changes occur today. Some, however, may come about later. But someplace along the line, you'll find—even if you've been deliberately saying "No way will this work,"—that a background surge of metaphysical energy has swept you onto a warm shore of positivity, and what seemed to be sure catastrophe, has turned out to be exactly what the doctor ordered. Despite your dark suspicions, chance and destiny have given you the go-ahead for positive personal growth in whatever way you choose to go.

May take a while to believe it, but as coincidences continue to pile onto lucky chances, eventually you'll realize that around you some kind of amazing intuition is doing it's cheerful work and you're getting the benefits.

By seeing actual events happening, you'll turn your life around from whatever state it was before into better than it ever was.

Before You Make Changes, What Should They Be?

Sound good? Sure does, yet before you decide to make changes in your personal existence, it might be a sound idea to decide what those changes should be.

Ask many people what they would like to do if they had *carte blanche* to change their lives, and they'll likely give vague answers like, "I'd like to win a million dollars," or "I want to be retired and sit in the sun." Naturally, there are a multitude of happy thoughts that people daydream about. That's fine. Thoughts like those are excellent. All you have to do is find out how to turn those thoughts into connections so that instead of dreaming about something, you can actually see it happen before your very eyes.

Make Sure You're Aiming the Right Way

So we come to personal goals which will make sure you're aiming the right way for your dreams to come true. Think for a moment or two about what you would want to be or would do if you were totally free to choose, without any manipulation by other people. Inevitably, as soon as you start to consider some delightful outcome, up comes a thought like, "But what will my spouse say and do if I quit my job, move to a tropical island, and decide to become an artist?"

Just for this instant, disregard everything except your personal idea. This is about what *you* want to do; what other people may think or do is superfluous during this view of your world.

Think about this as a perfectly valid notion. Then consider the results of the idea. What do you really want to be? If you had no responsibilities, no obligations, and no worries about your future, what would you do, where would you go, how would you handle your life?

Putting logic to one side, forget about where the money will come from. In this temporary castle in the air, pay no attention to anybody or anything that's holding you back from happiness. Hang on to this idea, and stop thinking about the fact that you know right now that maybe the rent's overdue, the kids are driving you crazy, the washer just sprang a leak, your boss hates you, your transport just gave up the ghost, and you're feeling like death warmed over.

A Bit of Effort, But You Can Do It

Takes a bit of effort to bring all that kind of wonderful thinking to mind and abandon the hassles, stresses, and aggravations for a moment or two but you can do it, if you think about it the right way. Here's a particular approach where the consequence is that life becomes easier for you, day by day.

While you were putting this concept together maybe your initial idea of getting out from under your problems and responsibilities went something like, "First I'd win the lottery, then I'd decide what to do next." But hold hard a moment: Perhaps you're a little on the wrong frequency band. *Ah, ha!* Your mind says, *thought there was a catch in it someplace.*

Well, it is a small stumbling block, and certainly positive thinking works a little differently from merely stating your requirements and then expecting bounty to fall from heaven. In point of fact, that kind of thing does happen, but it's very likely to be in some way that's totally unexpected.

So instead of baldly stating your demand, another way to set up this line of thinking is to form a picture, a very specific picture. We'll explore the how of this later, but, for the moment, enjoy the luxury of seeing your last wish come true, just as I outlined, with no strings and no hassles attached.

Enjoy the End Result

What next? You simply allow it to happen. See this delightful picture and enjoy the glorious end result. No need to fuss about the intervening steps. Exactly how this will all happen, you can safely leave to your destiny, your Inner Mind and coincidence.

By the way, using the words *Inner Mind* is a kind of shorthand for the combination of your subconscious and superconscious, but it might be easier to leave that concept to one side until we've explored later chapters of this book.

We'll, perhaps, deal with that pathway later, but right now let's return to the idea of allowing things to happen. What I'm suggesting you do is to think about that delightful outcome—your desired status.

For instance, if you define success as being wealthy, forget about any idea that you may have inherited a bundle from Uncle Fred after years of him saying he'd rather give his money to the local animal hospital. Instead, see yourself enjoying the fruits of a windfall, without you needing to spell out where the additional benefit comes from or whether you had to buy a ticket.

Reach Every Goal You Set Up

It's as simple as that. Be assured that you will inevitably reach every goal you set up for yourself—all you have to do is to create those goals in your mind. Naturally, with everyone having different targets and aims, what those goals are, is your personal choice, and that can be a fascinating project for a start.

So before you decide to change your life, it might be a favorable plan for you to consider what you might want to change it to. It's all very well to own a metaphorical magic wand and say, "Shazam! I have changed my life." That's fine, but now you've changed it, did it make a difference? If it *did* make a difference, is your life worse or better than it was before?

Of course, you naturally expected life to be better than before. How much better? Sure, in this imaginary place, you're rich, you're nobody's slave—or if you do have to work, you're working at something you truly enjoy—your health is perfect, in fact everything's perfect. That's fine.

But in this ideal picture, did you forget anything while you were waving your virtual magic wand? How about Uncle Zeke? In your ideal picture, is he still as irritating as ever? Right! Another twitch of your wand, and there went Uncle Zeke and his smelly pipe and know-all ways.

But of course, now that we've remembered him, there's young Kathy down the road. She's a pest more than anything else, even if she *is* heading for becoming a delinquent. But she certainly sullies the ideal picture you're painting. There must be a dozen or more people and things that bug you that you'd like to get rid of. Legally, of course.

Take A Look At That Perfect Picture

So here's an idea. Prior to you deciding to turn everything around to make you happy, content, and comfortable, perhaps it might be a worthy scheme to take a look at that perfect picture prior to it's creation. Then, before you wave your wand, you can be moderately sure you've got it right and it will be unnecessary to keep tweaking your wand for extra bits and pieces you've forgotten about.

So here's a list of stuff you might want to check off so that when you swing into action with synchronicity, nothing gets forgotten from the outset. What I'm offering you is a set of items, and with each item are a couple or so questions.

Sounds like an exam in school, right? May sound like it, but it's a lot more comfortable than any exam: This is a record of what's going to make you the most satisfied and contented person in the world.

Start With Material Things First

Here we go, then, starting with material things and moving up to more ephemeral stuff. First things first, of course. A high percentage of readers will start with—you guessed it!—money. Okay: Your special intuition that we'll discuss in later chapters can get you that.

So next question: How much money? Remember a million bucks can be small change these days. I recall a gentleman on the East Coast who won a million-dollar lottery a couple of years back. He loved it, naturally. Loved it so much that he splurged the lot in just over six weeks forcing him to go back to the condition he'd been in before he won. On welfare. So better up your sights if it's dollar bills you want. If it's just money you want, that's fine. By all means, carpet your rooms with dollar bills, fill your basement with gold nuggets, hide a fortune in quarters in your garage. But on no account should you tell anyone you've got all that money lying around. Despite the best efforts of your local police force, there are nasty people out there who might coldly pistol-whip you, back up a truck, and make off with your wealth, leaving you with a headache and a whole bunch of paperwork. And no money, except for the few hundred bucks you'd slipped into the coffee pot and the thieves missed.

Money is the root of all evil, right? Wrong! The Good Book says, "The love of money is the root of all evil," so go ahead, you can, if you wish, get all the money you wish in whatever way you wish. But what I am going to do is ask you another question.

What do you want this money for? Even assuming those thieves miss grabbing your coin, having all that money around can be a decided fuss. If you're going to buy something worthwhile, like a new truck, a bigger home, new furniture, or a world cruise, you're going to have to go to the trouble of spending the money, maybe tramping through the rain and cold to look at trucks, chatting with realtors and looking at house after house until you're dizzy, worrying whether the movers are going to scratch your new furniture as it comes into the house.

And even after you've gone through the hassle of buying your larger home, will the new furniture fit properly or will you be forever banging your hip against the surround-sound system? And the world cruise? Raining on your parade would be a shame, but make sure you know where the cruise is going—some places these days are less safe than they could be.

Money Can Cause Problems

Getting any sort of message here? Yes, I guess having lots of ready money is fine, but it sure can cause problems at times, and who needs problems when you're wealthy? Can I whisper an idea to you? I'm going to anyway, and you can think about it seriously.

Try it this way. In your perfect intuitional paradise, it's no problem to jump over the hassle of money and instead receive whatever you want without talking to the bank. In other words, think about the shiny new truck, the larger home, the new furniture and the world cruise, and then find yourself enjoying the goods and services without worrying about where they came from.

In your dreams? Right—that's exactly part of it, as you'll find out later in this book. But to return to where we were when we started salivating about the material wealth you can gain, what else would you like to have without strings attached?

We've looked at material things a bit in the previous paragraphs. What say we expand the list?

A Mental Exercise

Probably your biggest asset is your home. Now this is confidential. I'll mind my own business here, so baring your soul and making like an auditor has been scratching around in your credit rating is denied. All I want you to do here is to think about various things. Even writing them down is unnecessary. This is a mental exercise you're looking at, perfectly personal and private.

Consider your current home. Whether it's a mansion, cottage, mobile home, cardboard box, car, tent, jail cell, sleeping bag under the tracks, or any other place you choose to sleep in, are you content with your residence? Do you rent it or is it mortgaged to the hilt? Whatever you're thinking about right now as far as home is concerned, are you totally satisfied with it? If it entirely fits your current life-style, you can move on to the next section.

But if you want to change your home, you can rev up your new perceptions you're reading about and start things happening.

Next question: When you make your next move, what will it be? *Where* may be all right, but I'm asking the question *what*. Think about your next dwelling. It needs to be one you'll enjoy, but remember this

mental description is flexible. You can produce a neat synchronistic home and then if you find it has disadvantages, certain strokes of luck will make necessary changes for you.

Fixing the Picture in Your Mind

So right now look up from this book and consider what you'd like your next dwelling to be. House, apartment, lake-side cottage, penthouse, motel room, mansion, palace, bungalow, log hut, castle, igloo, duplex, fifth wheel. Your choice, but spend this moment fixing the picture in your mind. Got it?

So on to the next section. Where are you going to be when you choose that next residence? You're perfectly happy in the area where you live? That's also fine, and if your idea of *perfect* is merely almost perfect, that'll be excellent—we can fine tune any details around your home later.

But assuming you do want to move to another location, where is it going to be? City, country, suburbia, in the desert, in the rain forest, far from the madding crowd, in the metropolis, in North America, South America, Australia, Europe, in some other foreign land, on a luxury liner? Once again, give that idea brief thought and then let it be. The concept has been fixed along within the gears or wheels of time and that celestial helm is already pointing toward your intended goal.

Keeping It Simple

So there went the *what* and *where* of your home. How about other assets? Transport perhaps? Naturally if you're set on living in and owning something like a huge mansion and grounds you never bother to leave, perhaps you'll never ask for or need a Rolls Royce Silver Cloud or a Lamborghini. On the other hand, if you want to have a roving commission, a superior RV might fit your personal style. Keeping it simple, let's just think about wheels in general. You can dot the *I*s and cross the *T*s in your mind as you think about this whole concept.

Again sit back for a moment and think about a particular vehicle you'd like to go along with your chosen residence. Yes, a boat will fit, if you wish. Let's try again: anything that moves, Okay? Cast your mental glance at each item. Pick out something which grabs your attention.

The winged lady on the hood of the Rolls. The shiny chrome of the Harley. The British racing green Jag. The TV and surround sound in the s-t-r-e-t-c-h limousine. Got those? Good. I was about to write, "Next asset coming up," yet maybe that's now superfluous. My guess is that I've gotten you pointed in the right direction now, without me having to list every last thing you hanker after.

This Exercise Takes Only a Few Minutes

Remember this little exercise takes a few minutes, but you can zap from one end of your assets to another in a mental flash. And that's all this quick perception of truth, without conscious attention or reasoning, needs to bring things together in literally amazing ways. All you need to do is to look around your residence. Walk around inside it if you wish, going from room to room, taking a brief mental note of what you need to get rid of before you can replace it with something new and more inspiring. If there's a gaping space somewhere in your domain, think about what you need to fill it. And when you've done that, you've set up the material changes needed.

So what next?

Change Yourself First

One change that might be beneficial would be to try emotional or mental alterations, and it might be an excellent idea for you to change yourself first.

How do you do that small thing? Several ways are possible, but one way you could do it would be for you to first identify some drawback you have in yourself. Think about whether you're too noisy. Too quiet. Too aggressive. Too lazy. Too cowardly. Too anything. Surely you're less than totally perfect? So think about it: if you are perfect, then are you *too* perfect?

Spend a minute or two considering what you've just read about yourself. Then think what it would feel like if you reversed any trait you've been considering. All you have to do is just pretend that this element of your mind has been created. If necessary you can borrow a book of antonyms, words which are directly opposed to others in meaning. Thus, noisy becomes quiet. Aggressive turns into inoffensive. Lazy becomes ambitious. Cowardly becomes brave. Quiet becomes exciting. Deficient becomes abundant. Get the picture?

Once more, these are simple-mind pictures to consider briefly. They will sort out the elements of what's needed and what's discretionary, and up will come the right stance for your personal growth.

Changing Other People

Once you've become adept at trying the antonym game, without a doubt you'll start thinking about what you may wish to change about other people. In that case, read and inwardly digest the bit about karma, the law of cause, and effect regulating your future life.

Towards the end of this book you'll find out how destiny and your fate intermingle with this major learning experience to bring you exactly where you want to be without surrounding hassles. Synchronicity works in enigmatic ways to achieve your objectives, but those objectives should be something which has come about by coincidence, and your intentions should match with the desires of other people. Recall the thought in the previous chapter about the universe being simply an interacting cluster of energy, with everything knitting in place simultaneously. Yes, you can, if you wish, change someone else's existence, their ideas, their whole life pattern, but those changes should appear to be coincidental.

Lest you might be drooling about making people obey your slightest command, you can abandon any of those kind of notions: Nowhere in this text does it promise that you can practice some arcane discipline such as bringing young naked virgins to your bed space or some similar carnal practice. That's very old-fashioned and almost certainly chauvinistic, and your up-to-the-minute intuition works in a different way entirely.

A New Dimension of Thought

So before you start thinking about any of the above dealings, it would be a good idea to read and absorb Chapter 10, where we discuss that interesting concept of personal cause and effect.

Meanwhile, having discussed material, emotional and mental changes in and around you, the idea of spiritual progress will come to many. Now we're in a new dimension of thought. Spiritual by its very definition means non-material, so much of the stuff discussed here you'll see happening in inexplicable ways, much more mental or emotional than anything you can touch, smell, taste, see or hear. The changes most definitely occur, and you'll be glad of them, but they will rarely be instantaneous. Only in retrospect will you be able to say, "Well, who'd have thought that could have happened?"

As well as material prosperity, spiritual wealth is also guaranteed for you. Gaining spiritual prosperity is definitely an intangible gift: You'll recognize it more from the emotional charge you get rather than from any possession or material asset you gain.

New Worlds of Anticipation

For example, as you explore patterns that repeat in time energies, you may discover previously hidden talents of intuitive thinking. In other words, you can, if you wish, become a spiritual mystic and that will open new worlds of anticipation and pleasure. Without a doubt, you've come across advertisements on television or in magazines about the wonders some psychics can perform. You can do the same things, and better, when you latch on to what some people have called a wink from the cosmos. Opening up a spiritual link into the *Unseen* is straightforward, so instead of paying about three bucks a minute for psychic advice that may possibly be genuine, you can open up your own channel to produce guidance in your life or the lives of other people.

On the other hand, your spiritual gift may arrive as the ability to heal. Many people have that ability, whether it's to *heal* a child's bump on the knee or to cure something more critical. When your spiritual energies are awakened, you can automatically bring comfort and therapy to yourself, other people, animals, organizations, or the world.

One way or another, you can transport yourself into other planes of existence if that is your desire—and always remember that you're in charge. If you decide to decline any of the coincidental gifts at any time, the choice is yours entirely. And there's no warranty to lock you into a gift—you can take a rain check on any intuitive benefits anytime you wish.

As you'll have already surmised, these wonders sometimes come along a little later than you may hope. In this text, you'll discover ways and means of avoiding some of the obstacles that may be in your way.

And I'll guarantee you one thing: Most of those stumbling blocks are likely to be more in your mind than anyplace else. Stick around and read Chapter 3 to discover how obstacles can be turned into interesting challenges that can either be conquered or evaded altogether.

Step 2:

Make a *specific* plan first.

Chapter 3

Give Yourself Permission

Silence is the means of avoiding misfortune.

Believe Nothing I Tell You.
Try It, Prove it to Yourself. Then Believe It.

Probably the most vital step of the whole process of these mysterious coincidences is to learn how to give yourself permission to continue along this path of new self-awareness and change. That can be a surprising thought for some people.

Naturally you're excited with this project and you expect to receive the benefits in short order. Strangely enough, despite absorbing what these methods can do for you and how you can change your path in life, sometimes you can run into a metaphorical brick wall as you try to persuade some obstacles to move away.

How come? It's likely to be a psychological hang-up. For years your subconscious mind has been doing its thing, quietly getting on with your life, keeping you going. Without you having to do anything to help, your subconscious mind has done its vital energies, keeping you alive. Right now your heart is pumping pints of blood at the right temperature and pressure around your veins and arteries. Your chest is moving up and down allowing oxygen to flow into your lungs so your blood can carry its healing fluids to your body and brain. Automatically, your body exhales carbon dioxide when your oxygen supply has been depleted and fresh air flows into your lungs to keep the process going. Throughout your body, countless energies have been working hard, all designed to keep you alive and kicking.

Your Vital Energies

Some may know it as your autonomic nervous system. Whatever you label it, this is a network of nerves that controls any of your body tissues and organs which are under subconscious, rather than voluntary, control. Your heartbeat, digestion, breathing rate, hormonal and enzyme activities, gland secretions, and all the delicate chemical balances that maintain your body in a state of animation are all motivated by your subconscious mind.

Now, at a level deeper than your subconscious, your Inner Mind is also part of your body, mind, and soul equation. Your subconscious handles all the autonomic stuff while your Inner Mind has the task of keeping your psychological, physiological, and spiritual energies in balance.

Your Inner Mind does that pretty well, but it's a whole new ball game if anything takes place that metaphorically rocks your personal boat. Consider, for instance, what happens to your Inner Mind if you consciously and deliberately affect the established conditions that both the subconscious mind and Inner Mind have been maintaining. Assume you do something to yourself that changes the steady state which has been going on in your mind and body.

The first thing that happens is that your Inner Mind pays attention. "What's going on?" asks Inner Mind. "Things were going fine, so why make any changes?"

Your Inner Mind Tries to Keep Everything the Same

In fact, as far as your Inner Mind is concerned, anything that changes your existing state is cause for wariness and is likely to make your Inner Mind try to keep things the same. Hence, this idea of roadblocks that need moving out of the way.

No big deal. All you need to do is to take specific steps to have those roadblocks removed. The first way to try it is ultimately simple: All you should do is speak firmly but gently to your subconscious mind to give it your consent to go ahead. Weird? Just a touch—but it works.

Once you get all levels of your mind cooperating and accepting the theory of this book, your life will improve automatically and amazingly.

Setting Up A Phrase

So set up a phrase you affirm regularly whenever it's convenient and you remember it. Most especially you should say, murmur or think this phrase when you are doing any of the techniques and exercises from your intuitive peak.

This bit of business needs a little work as you try it. What you're aiming to do is to get your Inner Mind to cooperate, and you do that with a subtle *twist* of your conscious mind: You need to pretend that you and your Inner Mind are two separate entities. You, at your conscious thinking level, are going to speak to your Inner Mind. The fact that several levels of your mind are working within the same brain case is irrelevant. Try this bit of mind slanting and you'll be amazed at the result.

To get this effect working, think, in your mind (or aloud if you wish),

> "Listen, Inner Mind, please join us in a spiritual experiment. During this exploration, everything will remain as before and the entity which we are a part of will remain unchanged. Only our concepts will have altered."

Repeat that mind-produced, thought twice more.

Notice the fact that you refer to *us, we,* and *our* in your mind: a combination of all the neat stuff that goes on, and will continue to go on in remarkable ways.

Now for the mildly devious bit. You've spoken to Inner Mind; it has perked up its metaphysical ears, ready for words of wisdom or similar stuff to come moving through your brain into your subconscious. So? Poor old Inner Mind, who knows if it has a disappointment feature? Because as soon as you've mentally mentioned this experiment and Inner Mind has responded, the experiment has already been carried out!

So What Was the Experiment?

Well, for the sake of putting it all together, what exactly was the experiment and what was its purpose? Okay, the experiment was first to say three times the actual phrase that tweaked Inner Mind's understanding. Simply doing that got things moving: Inner Mind woke up to the effect that something was going on.

You'll know all about it as soon as you try to climb the wall that was in your way when you wanted to move on and found you were tied down by your own subconscious mind.

So now to the next step in your new awareness performance.

The Next Step

You'll have realized by now that part of this karmic concept suggests that you, the basic person who's thinking and reacting to these words, is a product of your own thoughts. You create or attract conditions by your personal decisions, actions, and reactions: Whatever you regularly think or imagine has a habit of coming true. Added to that hardly significant aspect, you have a much more remarkable gift.: It's the power to change anything in your environment, whether it's material, emotional, intellectual, spiritual, or truly mystical.

You can achieve that apparent lucky break by opening the doors of your deeper mind and allowing a whole raft of spiritual energy to come flooding in. Now despite your best efforts of using the thrice-stated phrase above, you may find subconscious resistance holding back your intuitive energy. But of course there are many ways of going through or around those self-imposed obstacles.

The first one which works for many people is by singing, chanting, murmuring or mentally reciting a particular phrase which, for the purpose of this section of the work, we can call a mantra. What the chant is doing is distracting your subconscious, and while that's going on, you can sneak a whole passel of energies into the equation.

A typical mantra can be *'Om-mani-padme-hum,'* a repeated phrase you may have heard elsewhere. It's Indian in origin but many other countries have phrases which can be used as mantras. J. H. Brennan in his book *Experimental Magic* mentions the Middle Eastern *'Hui allahu alazi lailaha illa Hua'* which translates into the somewhat male chauvinistic 'He is the One Divinity and there is no other Divinity but He.' The foreign version sounds prettier when chanted, but as far as Brennan is concerned, he (during a psychological experiment) successfully used an unusual mantra to see if it would work. It did. Far from being an obscure foreign phrase, his mantra was *Twinkle, twinkle, little star, How I wonder what you are.* Seems the words of the piece that you chant, sing or mutter are pretty innocuous perhaps meaningless and, long before Hallmark™, many people realized it's the thought that counts. You got that in mind? It's important.

You've Got Powerful Buddies

What you're doing there is putting on a show to distract your subconscious, and one production that also works well is to tell your subconscious you've got powerful buddies who will help.

Once again you announce to your Inner Mind what you're going to do, and it would probably help things along if you said the same things three times. As Lewis Carroll in *The Hunting of the Snark* said, "What I tell you three times is true," and that's a bit of occult ritual that can resound in your brain.

What you can do if you want to really impress your Inner Mind is to call on the celestial energies of nature sprites. Oh, come on! Sprites? They're imaginary beings out of fantasy land, right? Well, imaginary they may be, but they exist in this universe in some fashion or another. And a small part of this matter brings nature sprites into the picture in remarkable ways.

You're skeptical? Okay. Stop reading for a minute. Close your eyes and think about something that has been bugging you lately. Anything. That lost deal. Your partner's attitude. Your own attitude, perhaps. The gouge you found on your new paint work yesterday. Your headache. That plugged up washroom.

So you've thought about one of those problems briefly? Now think about a nature sprite. Any sprite you like will do the trick: in your mind's eye, see a pixie, one of the little people you've heard about in fairy tales. Conjure up such a being in your mind.

If you have trouble thinking about the shape, size, and posture of your nature sprite, think about a Walt Disney cartoon character. His pixies are exactly what you need. Think about this elf: notice the color of his or her outfit. And her hair? Dark or light or maybe shining red? Many sprites are blonde and without doubt bright as a new-minted penny. In particular, you should spot her sassy little smile. And if you can see her turn to you and wink (maybe with just a touch of a smirk), this could be the start of something big.

Whatever goes on there, once you've managed (however slyly) to think pixie, make a note on your scratch pad that that's what you've done. Then remember it again in twenty-four hours. Amazing chances are that what was bugging you yesterday is no longer a problem. A sprite did it for you? Who knows? But you'll see the results, even though you may be dubious about the means.

Four Archangels

As you may recall in the introduction to this book, I used to call on the four Archangels to work this kind of technique. They never got annoyed as far as I can recall, but now I use less significant energies to perform my tasks.

Here you're looking at having a nature sprite help you remove obstacles, so Puck, Shakespeare's merry wanderer of the night, would probably do nicely, unless he's busy, in which case mercurial Eshu who is the equivalent of the Joker in the Tarot cards, would probably be available.

Remember, this is all imagination, but somehow it works. Your sprightly summons might be something as simple as just naming your sprite, announcing his or her name three times and visualizing your pixie sitting beside you. Something a little more elaborate would be adding a bit more energy to the session by adding a phrase like "Yo, Eshu (or whatever name you choose for your sprite) please carry out my request." Remember the triple statement, be nice to your sprite and thank him or her when you've finished.

Of course, if you're into stuff like Wicca or similar enchantment, you could put on a magnificent show for your Inner Mind by you performing some ritual magic. But unless you're a magical expert, that might take more time and study than you wish to understand and absorb at this time.

But while we're on the subject of magic and the occult, you may find that even with your best efforts to get rid of obstacles, things are working out differently from the way you wish them to.

Company Trouble

Could be you've got some negative energy getting in your way. I recall years ago a U.S. publisher telephoning me when he was having trouble with his company. He told me that a book he was trying to publish was having all kinds of problems and it would be running late "because he was under psychic attack."

Now that's a whole new ball game as far as synchronicity is concerned. If you're *au fait* with the term, and things are falling apart in some way, it could be that you yourself are under psychic attack. I mention this for the sole purpose of completeness: Being under a psychic attack is extremely unlikely. Most alleged psychic attacks are nothing of the kind; they're mostly imagination run wild, or perhaps they're the product of an inflated ego.

If you really are having a psychic attack, one deliberately produced by an adept of the occult arts, you'll know about it. Dion Fortune in her book *Psychic Self-Defence*, a study in occult pathology and criminality, says: "if there is a definite psychic attack . . . there will soon begin to appear characteristic dreams."

Horrid Dreams

Those dreams may feel as if someone is kneeling on the dreamer's chest, or the attack can result in absolute-horror dreams that last well through breakfast time.

Despite Stephen King and similar dreadfulness writers, true psychic attacks are rare. Mind you, if you've chosen to join a Black Magic circle, or to do similar negative kinds of things, maybe using voodoo and sorcery, you may be targeted. But frankly, if you choose to get into that kind of stuff, you'll deserve everything that happens to you.

The Right Direction

What we're looking at here is doing things right for yourself without anything more than tweaking synchronicity in the right direction so that what you want to get becomes a reality.

But apart from negative influences, there certainly are other energies which can keep you chained to your material wall of trouble and keep you away from your most cherished desires and needs.

From People Close To You

Those energies are perfectly everyday in nature: They come from people close to you who are negative in thought, word, and deed. There are plenty of those around, as you well know: Listen almost anytime and many of the folk you talk to will allege that they're having problems in life.

Temporarily Wading Through Molasses

Words have powers of their own and anytime anyone announces or even thinks a negative, someone gets a blast of destructive energy that can metaphorically set them back on their heels, at least temporarily. And if that person happens to be you as you're setting up to do some angel creation effect, inevitably you'll feel you're temporarily wading through molasses as you begin this great work.

So what can you do to combat negativity? First things first. Calling a halt to saying negative things and words would be a good start. When you hear yourself ready to make a negative statement, stop and rearrange the phrase so you disregard it, and instead say it someway else so you don't use it.

Now, were you listening during that last sentence? I deliberately dumped in a downbeat concept to see if you were paying attention. "So you don't use it" would have been better stated as: "so that it's affirmative." Thus an assertion, "It doesn't work," could be stated: "Maybe it will work tomorrow."

Using positivity regularly is truly a mind game, and some negatives can really be positives. If you're going to play this game, it might perhaps be easier to clean out all negatives rather than roll around the floor spending time deciding if a particular negative is positive.

True or False?

You can also spend energy uselessly when you run into paradoxes. For example, think of the simple phrase, "I always tell lies." Is that statement true or false? If the speaker is lying, in this case he or she has told the truth, so the statement is a lie. Forget it—you can think yourself blue in the face and still have no firm answer when sorting out contradictions like those. But while we're at it, a few four-letter words could be thrown out so you avoid some of the inevitable negativity that arrives when you use them. Three of the words are *pain, sick* and *hate*: If you can manage to use other words instead of those three whenever you think or talk, you'll be doing yourself a metaphysical favor.

And next time someone says to you "that's difficult" or "that's going to be a problem" notice as the conversation progresses how the odds are stacked against an easy solution. If either phrase can be changed to "a challenge," instead of "difficult" or "problem," the negative energies drift away and more positive conditions develop. That's just a minor proposal, but you might say in this respect that every little helps.

Let's turn back to the subject in hand: synchronicity and your specific speech patterns. Apart from watching those negative words, you can go a long way to helping causal coincidence by walking away from anyone who consistently wants to tell you bad news. You can easily recognize the doomsayers in your life, and it would be a splendid idea to find the positive folk around you Join them, and listen to them, rather than being one of the Cassandras of this world (fer heavens sake, there are more than enough of those around!).

Who's Cassandra? She comes from Greek mythology, a daughter of Priam, and she was a seer who said something uncool about Apollo. He thus perpetually screwed up Cassandra's prophecies so that although they always came true, nobody ever believed what she said, and that's somewhat distressing for your average soothsayer. Over the years, a *Cassandra* has become known as someone who makes useless predictions of calamity.

Positive Affirmations

In a few words, what will help your motivational energies will be to replace any negative statements in your life with positive affirmations. As I already pointed out in Chapter 1, a very useful affirmation is Mr. Coué's early memorable assertion about "better and better." Some affirmations are easy to handle: "I can do it," replaces "I can't." "I'm not smart enough to grasp this" easily becomes "I'm bright enough to handle this." "I'm too old" needs a little care: If you indeed either are too old or you think you are, try an affirmation that says, "I'm just right for this project." "I can't change the way I am," needs to be altered to "I can solve this." Enough, already!

You can state your affirmations whenever you have time, and having time is the important thing. As you go about your daily life pay attention to what you should be doing, whether it's driving a car, reading a book, composing a symphony, designing computer software, teaching your child or any other of the tasks of this stressed life most of us live 24/7. Affirmations come after your list of must-dos: You should rarely feel that affirmations come first on the list. If you can personify the affirmations, you can say they'll accept their role at the bottom of the totem pole. They will then work better than as if you try to state them and then feel guilty because you had to postpone something else in order to take the time to listen to these mundane (but most important) words and phrases.

Best Time

Even if you seldom have a single moment to think about affirmations during your day, there's one time when they will come into their own and prove to be more than usually effective.

That time is just before you go to sleep. All you have to do is remember one or more of your affirmations and repeat the words in your mind as you are drifting into sleep. The closer you drift into the arms of Morpheus, the god of dreams, as you sleepily state your affirmation, the more your words will reach down from your conscious to your subconscious or Inner Mind and drill them into your soul.

The First Thought

Next morning, as you realize you're waking up, grab the first thought which drifts up into your mind as you awaken. You may latch on to a whole dream sequence. You may merely get a single word, yet as you dash to the bathroom that word may blossom into a complete dream. On the other hand, you may only get a feeling that you dreamed something even though your best attempts at recall fail, as you try to figure exactly what that something was.

In that case, consider the kind of *flavor* of your dreams at the moment you awoke. What did you feel? Anger? Fear? Happiness? Anticipation? Frustration? Bleh? As you think about this *flavor* of your dreams, consider what your dream may be telling you.

A Simple Record

If you wish, you can keep a dream journal beside your bed so that you can scribble down the highlights of your dreams. It needs to be nothing exotic; an ordinary exercise book will do nicely. Instead of a journal by Samuel Pepys, this is going to be a simple record purely about your dreams. Keeping such a chronicle over weeks and months can give you valuable input into what your subconscious is doing.

Unless you're one of the people who dreams true—a person whose dreams show exactly what your subconscious is saying to you—you'll find your dream journal persistently brings up particular symbols or events.

From those symbols, you can recover useful data, once you recognize what those symbols mean. Remember, these symbols are yours and yours alone, nobody else's.

Purely for fun, you can check one of those books of dreams or check an online website for dream interpretation. For example, one dream book says that if you dream of a carrot, it signifies that you have a great deal of work to be done and you'll get little reward for it. Or if you dream of cutting a cabbage, it means that a close companion is envious of you. Yes, those things can be amusing, but the real benefit of keeping a dream journal is to discover and interpret your own personal symbols.

Valuable Tips

Any time you find match-ups and recurring situations in your dreams, you can get valuable tips about your present, or even your future, whether it's about the next day or even years hence.

Typically, my partner used to have a recurring dream that made no sense to her for years. It was, of all unlikely things, just a partial picture of forget-me-not flowers, and whenever this dream surfaced, she always felt as if she was saying, "This is it!" The picture had been lying dormant in her mind for a long while, until the pair of us had gone house-hunting.

You no doubt know about that sort of annoyance, seeing houses day after day, some being sort of okay, others being no good at all. Luckily, we had a very patient realtor as we viewed and rejected house after house. Then we hit pay dirt. The realtor had opened the door of a vacant house, and she and my partner and I had walked into the hall.

"This is it!" my spouse said, "Where do we sign the offer?"

The realtor was amazed. "Don't you want to see over the rest of the house?"

"No, thanks, that's unnecessary," my partner said, "I told you this was it. I'm uncertain why this is, but I know we've reached the end of this particular trail for now."

She was right. The deal was struck and we soon moved in to our literal dream house.

It was more than a year later that my partner's dream dropped into place. She had been wondering if we should be doing some decorating in the main bedroom of our home. She had been looking at the wallpaper in the end suite washroom.

"I've found my dream symbol," she said to me. "Right there." She pointed up at the corner of the room. There was a portion of wallpaper showing a field of forget-me-nots.

After that, her recurring symbol quit cold. It had served its purpose and had been scrapped onto the astral garbage pile. That's one way of using symbols, and they come in all shapes, sizes, and manners.

Ask Questions

For example, I know whenever I'm dreaming that I'm traveling in a vehicle, I should think about the surroundings of the dream and ask myself questions. In the dream, I must ask if I'm controlling the car, truck, snowmobile or whatever, or is someone else handling the controls?

If I'm driving, I know that my subconscious is saying, in effect, "Go ahead with whatever you're planning because you're on the right track." But if someone else is driving the vehicle, I know that I must be careful, in the real world, to watch for an event which is taking me in a direction that someone else may be pushing me, and that direction may be the pits.

I recall a dream when I was sitting on a bus with a bunch of strangers. The vehicle was going fast downhill to some unknown destination and I was uncertain about where I was going to end up.

I've learned better now, but at the time I missed the symbolism of my dream. The bus driver was in control, and I was merely a passenger. In the real world, despite the dream warning, I decided to move from the east to the far west of the U.S. and get involved with a new project with a group of people I'd met only by telephone. Suffice to say, it worked out unsuccessfully and it took many months before I was again firmly on track in my line of work.

Future Paths

I've found, over the years, that my subconscious can unerringly notice future paths, and those clues have enabled me to do things better than I might have done if those Inner Mind tip-offs had been absent. You can do the same if you wish.

But whatever you dream, remember it's the symbol in the dream that's important; the actual dream picture itself, even if it's in Technicolor™ and stereophonic sound, is another matter.

For example, my daughter, Viki, used to dream about insects at times. The best she could come across in dream interpretation books was that the dream reflected something irritating or bugging her, or perhaps she had a feeling that she was unimportant. That hardly seemed to apply to her life and psychology, and it was only many years later that Viki recognized the dream.

The Inner Mind is an interesting place indeed: the bugs in her dream had no real connection or relevance to anything except that whenever the bugs appeared in Viki's dream, she would be prompted to call her mother and find out if everything was all right at home. Anytime her *bug dream* appeared, some daughter-to-mother connection was made which had Viki say, "Hey, Mom, I had the bug dream last night. Are you okay?"

Invariably, this tied into a health matter, and Viki, a Reiki master and teacher, would send Reiki energy to my wife to help heal the malady.

I recall one time when Viki called to inquire about the latest *bug dream* she'd had, and during the conversation, she commented, "they were enormous bugs." Within two days my wife had to go to hospital for fairly major surgery.

Solve Some Puzzles

So you can see that dreams, although often hard to make out, can help to solve some of the puzzles in this Universe.

But while we're mentioning dreams, how about negative dreams, where you wake up bathed in sweat after a nasty nightmare has been twitching at your mind. Or even those kind of dreams which are less than true nightmares, but still leave you feeling uneasy? Everybody has those kind of disturbances in their dream state, but if you're someone who suffers from unknown fears that disturb your waking and sleeping, here's something you can do that will help you.

Recognize Your Fears

By focusing in on your dreams, whatever their subjects and character, you can find out what it is you fear. And once you've got a handle on exactly what your apprehension is, you can get rid of it.

This technique is tied into your dream journal. Earlier I suggested you keep such a record and if that's what you did, now's the time to turn the pages.

To discover what your fears are, record one of your dreams as soon as you wake in the morning. Pay no further attention to the dream; in fact, it would be a good idea to close your notebook as soon as the dream has been recorded. No peeking! Whatever the dream sequence was, ignore it for the moment and merely go about your regular routines all day. Then, just before you're ready to go to bed, and before you've looked at your dream journal again, write down whatever you recall of that day's dream.

Now you can open your notebook. Take the time to compare the morning dream with this later sequence. Naturally you'll have forgotten parts of the dream: you'll realize that until you did this comparison a whole chunk of the dream was wiped from your memory during the day.

That's a typical subconscious ploy: whatever you've forgotten, your Inner Mind is trying to conceal. So by bringing this concealed stuff up to the surface, you'll become better attuned to all levels of your mind, especially your subconscious.

The first part is easy. You read your dream journal for that morning and identify the part of the dream that created the fear. So that identifies the specific symbol (which could be an actual event) that caused the fear. Next you use a recognized synchronicity technique to break your emotional links to the fear.

Getting Rid of Nightmares

Anything may symbolize a fear, but often it's some kind of monster, or it's a situation where you're terrified and something horrible is creeping up on you. Getting rid of such nightmares is a good idea, and just as many psychiatrists say you should face down your nightmares, so you can do that yourself when you get good at dreaming.

Next time your monster in your subconscious suddenly snarls at you and threatens to tear you limb-from-limb, create a corresponding anti-fear which will bring your monster to heel.

You can learn to control and shape your dreams so that you kind of write the script while you're sleeping. It's fun, and when you do that, your monster of the night can literally turn into a dream kitten (provided you're unaffected by cat hair). Or you can build yourself an impregnable fortress where you can live happily ever after while your nightmares grumble and growl outside.

One person I know used to banish nightmares by dreaming herself to be a magician with a cloak and staff, holding a wand that shriveled up any fearsome creatures of the night.

Holding on to the Memory

Learning to control and shape your dreams is a learned art, and first, you need to get the hang of recognizing dream sequences and holding on to the memory of them after you wake. One way to do that is, just as you're drifting into the fuzzy area between waking and sleeping, you say to yourself something like, "Please let me see my dreams, remember them, and then control them." A few nights of doing that little ritual will do wonders for your dreams, and fairly soon, you're likely to read in your dream record: "Managed to change my dream by myself."

From there on in it gets easier and easier. Eventually, anytime you're into a dream, you'll know at some level of your being that if something is different from the way you want it to be, you just make it happen, and there you are—deep into a dream that is going exactly the way you want it to be. I'll leave it to you to decide precisely what those fascinating dream sequences will be.

Here Comes Astral Travel

And once you get involved in the marvelous area of dreams, one special day you'll wake up and recall that you've been on an astral journey.

Now, if you've ever wondered about astral traveling (also know as OOBE's—out-of-body-experiences) and thought you might try it, you're almost halfway there when you try the technique of making dreams go your way.

Yet even before you check out astral journeying, there's a mental state and condition that you'd be well to experience, because one of the challenges that holds you back from astral traveling is the whole illogical idea that you have at least two areas of being. You consist of a physical body—that's easy. But you also have a part of you that can be detached, and that's your astral body.

Seeing your physical body is simple, but seeing your astral body needs a particular merge of your mind. Now if you could actually see your astral body, using your regular eyes, instead of what some mystics call your *Third Eye*, your mind would have to accept the truth and reality of astral travel, and that would make your path easier.

So here's a technique that enables you to literally see part of your astral body, and that way your mind will accept the actuality of astral journeying.

Seeing Your Auric Sheath

Your astral body is a challenge to see, but your Auric Sheath which is part of your astral body is fairly easy to observe.

Maybe fifteen minutes of looking will convince you of your Auric Sheath's reality. The first thing you should do is to darken the room somewhat; then sit down in a comfortable chair and watch the show.

Raise your hands in front of you, palm to palm, somewhat as if you're praying. Now move your hands about a quarter-inch apart. As you do that, look between your palms to the end of the room. You'll get a double image of your hands as you look beyond them but move them around so that you can see between them with at least one eye. You should now be paying attention to the inner palms of your hands but at the same time looking through them.

Continue to watch your hands. Blink when you need to, and you'll begin to see a haze of change moving over your palms. You may see a blue-gray layer of mist between your palms. Keep looking through your hands, keeping your gaze focused at the end of the room but keeping your attention on your hands. You're seeing the gray haze of your auric sheath, your auric body that's part of your astral body.

Now turn your hands so your fingers are pointing towards each other, with your second fingers almost touching. Again look between your fingers to the end of the room and watch for a haze to form between your finger tips. You'll see your Auric Sheath again as the grayish film you saw between your palms.

Seeing that phenomenon has given your Inner Mind and conscious mind an important proof that separation of the physical and astral bodies is possible. You'll also know, at some inner level, that you are ready and able to make this separation.

You might like to practice that hand exercise in various lighting conditions: you'll most likely see your auric sheath most clearly when you're in a dim light. If you wake up one morning just at dawn, when it's still too dim to see printing on a newspaper, but you can distinguish the outline of your bedroom door, that's when you're most likely to get the auric sheath effect. And once the auric sheath is clear both in your body and mind, you can simply swing yourself into an astral journey.

If you're heading up that particular metaphysical path, using your dreams as I mention in this chapter and also practicing your Auric Sheath manifestations, both are excellent ways to move into astral traveling and a bonus is that they're also excellent ways of getting your destiny working full force.

A Remarkable Trip

Initially, an astral expedition is likely to begin spontaneously, and that's definitely a remarkable trip in itself. Author Dion Fortune says simply that an astral journey is a particularly vivid experience, similar to dreaming. Swami Panchadasi suggests it's much more than that: He says during astral travel, part of you leaves your body for distant places and you are actually at those places with all your senses working.

You Are Somewhere Else

Whatever an astral journey is subjectively, you will experience it as a voyage of your awareness outside of your physical body, with the journey taken in full conscious control whenever you wish. Your physical body lies as if you're sleeping while you—the thinking, remembering, feeling, and experiencing you—are somewhere else.

And it's effortless. Everyone can astral travel. You do it when you're fully asleep. What synchronicity can do is help you master the art of astral traveling at any time, and bring you clear memories of what went on at the particular destinations you've chosen.

Why Travel Astrally?

Good question! Well first, it's fun. But secondly, it's a very useful discipline of the mind. It's basic work for many other intuitive and occult arts, including channeling, ritual magic, reincarnation research, exploring the future and, of course, shaping your own future by applying psi-related procedures.

How to Astral Travel

First things first. The astral plane is a new place for you to explore, so take this trip just as you would if you have gone to a city or a forest where you've never been before. If you choose to rush along, totally unprepared, you'll probably be puzzled, lost, and disoriented in no time at all.

So initially, the best thing for you to do is to investigate slowly. Whether you're going to a new city or to the astral plane, it will be a good plan to locate yourself a firm home base and then explore around it, just like the first astronauts did on the moon. It's probably best for you to walk before you try to fly.

Gently Does It

So here we go to gently master the ability of sliding out of your physical body and letting your awareness roam free.

But before we start, your question may be, "Is astral travel dangerous?" The answer is definitely in the negative. Despite anything you may have been told or read about it, astral traveling is about as hazardous as going to sleep at night. Your challenge will be to stay *out there* because any disturbance to your physical body will bring you zapping back to the mundane world in a split second. Nobody gets stuck out there, and you'll never return from a journey to find another soul is occupying your body.

Many Legends

When it comes to astral travel there are many legends and falsehoods about the practice which is, after all, a sort of deep sleep, as far as your body is concerned. It's your mind that gets the airing, yet some practitioners fence astral journeying around with a whole field of fears and misconceptions. Which is a pity because an astral journey can be a marvelous involvement rather than a fearful nightmare.

Some astral travelers who have written about the phenomenon have leaned on the sensational side and explained all manner of unlikely things.

Even genuine investigators, such as Robert Crookall who wrote that *The Techniques of Astral Projection* refers to astral travelers encountering adverse influences. Crookall mentions *mockers* which seem to be apparitions which result in a sense of fear and revulsion. Oliver Fox, an occult researcher who wrote a book in the 20s called *Astral Projection* refers to a warning pain that can become so excruciating that your astral journey is terminated abruptly. Edward Peach, another researcher of Inner Plane phenomena who calls himself Ophiel, refers to things that go bump in the astral, resulting in strange sounds and voices that occur in your astral voyaging, and as Ophiel himself says, "these noises are going to scare you and maybe scare you good." And Cyril Henry Hoskin, an author who preferred to be named Tuesday Lobsang Rampa, referred in his book *You-Forever* about strange astral beasties that slobber and drool and put on strange horrifying expressions when you're astral journeying.

What May Happen?

So it's hardly surprising that when you take a look at astral tripping, you're likely to be already apprehensive about what may happen during your journeys. And that's a great pity because as Benjamin Franklin said, "The only thing to fear is fear itself." That's especially true when it comes to exploring the Unseen.

Yes, I hear you: what about Lobsang Rampa? He was the man who wrote a karmic contract to make a soul exchange so that his awareness and someone else's took over each other's souls, right? Well, that's what Rampa said he did, but the jury's still out as to whether that actually happened, and seeing the *Old Man* died in Calgary, Canada, in January 1981, we may have to ring the bell on the Pearly Gates to get answers.

Never Lost An Astral Traveler Yet

All I can suggest to you is that I've run a lot of astral travel seminars in my time, and to my knowledge, none of my astral travelers have yet been lost!

Forget the nay-sayers, take the plunge: it's easy and non-threatening, and you can quit anytime you feel the trip is getting out of hand in any way.

First you need a place to begin your research. A room would be best for a start, someplace where you'll be undisturbed for a while. Unplug the phone, hit the *power off* button on your cell, tell your computer to suspend any beeps as your e-mails come in. Switch off the radio, the TV, and any other electronic gadgets that may disturb you in the next half-hour or so. I nearly suggested you put a *Do Not Disturb* notice on your doorknob, but I realize that would be tempting fate. Hang that sign in your residence and within minutes someone will tap on the door and ask, maybe in a whisper, "Why are you putting that thing on your door?"

Take A Walk

Having got rid of interruptions, somehow you've managed to get things as quiet as possible.

Now stand up and look around you. Look at your feet, feel the shape of your body. Then take a slow walk around your room. Put one foot in front of the other, and notice it happening. Walk just a few steps, a gentle amble from one place to another. While you're doing that, look around you, quietly. Whatever catches your gaze, stop and look at it. Could be your calendar, a poster on the wall, a book, your computer, even a crack on the wall. Take your time and remember the items that caught your attention. This should take you about quarter of an hour or more. Finally, finish your walk and return to the position you were in when you started this minor workout.

Try Relaxation

In Chapter 6, there will be an explanation on full relaxation, but for the purposes of this exercise, you do not need that kind of depth. (Later you may find it beneficial to relax like an old sock before doing any metaphysical exercise.)

So if you're going to do full relaxation later, at this time, sit in a recliner or on a mattress and get comfortable. Close your eyes and think about the room tour you've just taken. Replay the walk in your mind, recalling what you saw, felt and heard. In your mind, pretend you are observing yourself doing this. Ask yourself how you feel. Are you finding, even if it's only for an instant, the feeling that you're in two places at once? If so, that's wonderful—it's known as bi-location and inevitably that remarkable feeling will tiptoe over you sometime when you're practicing astral travel. If there's no sensation of bi-location, no need to lose any sleep about it for now. Later will be soon enough to get that odd, exhilarating feeling.

Open Your Eyes

Now open your eyes, but stay relaxed. Look straight ahead of you, then after a thirty- to forty-second count, close your eyes again. The brief break during this routine allows your mind to clarify and recall the different segments of this early astral mission.

Now remember your trip around your room and pretend you're doing it again, but this time head for a door. In your mind open the door and step outside your room. Notice the frame of the door as you move through it and pretend you're outside your room. Start a slow and steady walk through any other rooms you encounter until you reach the outer door of your building. On the way there look around you in your imagination. Who's in the building right now?

What are they doing? Do you see any animals, like pets perhaps, in the building? Does anything else strike you as interesting before you decide to open the outside door and step out into the open air?

Look Around

Notice the change of light as you move outside, feel air currents around your skin, taste the air, listen to any noises around you, feel any temperature change. Look around you. What do you see? If there are any parked cars close to you lean over and pretend you can read a license plate. Look down and see if anybody has left a newspaper on the sidewalk or on a bench, anywhere. If so, read the headline.

You've no doubt been this way many times, so as you're gazing around, look for anything unusual, something out of the ordinary that's changed since you were last here. Keep looking—you'll find something, even if it's only a toothpick someone threw down.

And when you've strolled along the street enough, turn around and replace your steps. Back to the front door of your building, inside and back through your door to your base astral traveling room.

Once you're back in your room, open your eyes and stand up beside your relaxing place. Recall what has been going on. Did you recall a license plate, a newspaper, anything unusual? Make a note of it.

Now for the brass ring. Physically and actually walk out of your room and walk outside, and in actuality notice the change of light and other stuff that you pretended to do in your mind trip.

Been Here Before?

Do you see anything special? That license plate you thought about in your mind, is it actually there in the mundane world? Can you read it? Likewise with newspapers or anything else, like posters or announcements—do you get a feeling of recognition, as if you've been here before as you stroll down the street?

In conclusion, walk back to your traveling room, sit yourself comfortably again and tell yourself: "I've just tried an astral journey. Thank you, Inner Mind."

We'll have a lot more to say about your Inner Mind as we continue, but for the moment, the experiment is over and you can move to whatever you were intending to do next. You can do this simple exercise anytime it's convenient. As you get proficient at it, you

can get more ambitious. Take a trip in your mind across your town, pretending you're flying. You can look out for unusual happenings in the town below you, and return to your astral traveling place when you're ready. One day, sooner or later, you'll know your astral journey is for real. You'll start feeling that sensation of bi-location fully, as you know perfectly well you're lying on your recliner, yet you can see the town below and describe what's going on at that time.

Where Can You Go When You're Astral Journeying?

And where can you astral travel to? Literally anywhere. When you're astral traveling you're using your astral body, while your physical body is in a state of relaxation. Your astral body needs no air to breathe for instance, so explore inside mountains, swim under oceans, tour the moon and other planets. Walk into buildings: seeing and experiencing the sights anywhere is your astral goal. And a hint for later in this book: as well as being able to fly and feel the wind on your face, you can astral travel in time—into the past or the future to find out what was or what will be.

All of these wonders, and many more, are yours to experience and carry out. Synchronicity will generate them for you, and as you continue to absorb this chapter you'll realize how simple and effortless it can be.

So why was I making such a big thing about astral qualms earlier in this chapter? Simple: it's because fears, whether they're real or imaginary, can stop both your astral journeying and meaningful chance from working properly, so if you can quell any incipient doubts, you'll be doing yourself a major favor.

What Would happen If...

You see, often a fear is created merely by the 'what-would-happen-if' syndrome. What would happen if the steering on your car suddenly broke down? That's a genuine fear that can prevent you from driving.

Other 'what would happen if' situations can bring fear of flying, fear of going out, or fear of a multitude of happenings. If you have irrational fears, they're called phobias, and my handy-dandy dictionary has no less than forty-eight phobias, ranging from fear of

aloneness (autophobia) to fear of noise (phonophobia) through to fear of animals (zoophobia), and there are lots more if you try one of the big dictionaries in your local library.

Imagination Experiment

Sorting out your dreams and finding out what's rational and what's irrational among your personal fears can help. But remember that the vast majority of fears are tied into your imagination. Try an experiment, if you will. Find, if you can, a couple of two-by-two inch wooden blocks, or maybe a pair of common house bricks will do. Any firm flat objects which you can put on the floor about five or six feet apart will do nicely. Next you'll need a stout board about six inches wide and about six feet long. Lift the board and put it on the two bricks. Make sure it's quite firm, without wobbling. Step up the couple of inches onto the board and walk along it.

Okay? No problem to walk the plank like that, is there? Step down and think about what you've done. Then close your eyes and pretend that you're about to step on the same board and walk along it, but this time, in your mind, pretend that instead of the board being balanced on a couple of bricks, it's suspended across a canyon, with a yawning hundred-foot drop to jagged rocks down below. Whoops!

Unless you're one of those people who regularly walk the steel around skyscrapers, or you're a tight-wire performer, you'll feel an instinctive twinge of fear even before you start to put the first foot on this make-believe board.

And that's the end of that experiment. Simple, but effective: you can now see how your mind controls you, unless you learn to take charge of it. While you're considering that important point, you can schlep the plank and blocks or bricks back into the shed and get back to reading this narrative. At the least it was good exercise.

That Imaginary Step

So what's with this game? First, I'll tell you the plank and blocks were only stage dressing. What we were looking for was the twinge of alarm you felt when you took that imaginary step out into the wide-blue yonder. That small feeling of distress came, you now know, purely from your thoughts. Dreams are the same, and now that you've understood the difference between imagination and real life, you'll find your dream sequences will become clearer and more interesting. Why that happens is an enigma. Maybe accept it as a *given*. Better—try it for yourself.

But I hear wails of distress at the back of the room. And I know what you're going to say next. "How can I get into one of those exciting dreams, when I know I dream once in a blue moon?"

Perhaps You Never Remember Your Dreams

I'll make a suggestion. It's very unlikely that you never dream. What happens I suspect is that, for some reason or another, you don't remember your dreams.

If you can recall your dreams, then you'll be amazed to discover what a fascinating world has been slipping away from you as soon as you go to sleep. Some metaphysical folk deliberately train their subconscious so that they can virtually have two existences. By day, they watch their world go by in the material plane, and then, as soon as they zap off into Zee-land, they start their dream world experiences. And believe you me, the average dream world is about a hundred times more exciting and satisfying than the average daily round when you're awake.

If you think about them, you'll realize that you experience dreams as if they are real events, but you recall dreams only when they've been clothed with suitable symbols by your mind.

Dreams Are Messages

But whatever dreams are, they are certainly messages from within, and if you can understand those messages, you're very fortunate because dreams most often consist of warnings, suggestions, or some kind of useful comment brought up into your brain.

Dreams come in at least four types. Typically you can dream about a previous event, and if you can sort out the dream story, you may find your subconscious is making suggestions on how you may better handle the event if it occurs again. You can call that a *Type One* dream. Most of your dreams, about sixty percent, will be of that variety.

Type Two dreams consist of advice on solutions to existing problems you may be having. Twenty percent of your dreams will be like that: You could call them inspirational dreams. This type of dream can be very useful. When you've got a particular challenge

taking place, tell yourself before you drift into sleep that you will dream a solution. Many times, as you awaken, you'll know perfectly well that you've dreamed the answer to your problem.

A smaller percentage of dreams, about twelve percent, will be *Type Three* dreams, and they'll consist of warnings of existing conditions. They'll take some sorting out because they'll be carefully disguised by your subconscious, but often the cautionary dreams are connected with medical conditions, your survival circumstances, or your personal conduct. Typically a *Type Three* dream will be telling you that, at that moment, you're heading in the wrong direction in your life (as I mentioned in my own example earlier) or, very mundanely, maybe it's time to visit your dentist.

And *Type Four* dreams, which come up only about eight times in every one hundred dream sequences, are the truly intriguing ones. They give you pictures and narratives of coming events. J. W. Dunne's book, *An Experiment with Time,* that I mentioned earlier in Chapter 1, examines how dreams are often precognitive. In other words, when you dream, you can look forward in time to get clear indications of what's going to happen in your future.

We'll be discussing that fascinating ability later on in Chapter 9, but meantime keep the idea in mind until we can discuss it more fully and use it to your advantage.

How To Recall Your Dreams

So how do you learn to recall your dreams?

As I suggested earlier, you need to get into the habit of recalling the very first notion that blossoms in your mind as you know that you're awake. It can be a thought, an impression, or even a picture, but as you realize that you're waking, something in your mind will tweak the thought. If you lose it at once, so be it—try it again. In fact, try the process each night for a month. Why? Because if your dreams come and go spasmodically, you'll find that at some phase of the moon, your mind will be much more attuned to what's going on subconsciously. That's the time in the month when you'll likely get your dream sequences. Note it in your diary and see how this cycle of the moon helps to bring your Inner Mind closer to your waking mind.

So what else can you do to help things along in your quest to using synchronicity?

Music Can Help

The whole idea here is to get your mind into a state where you can reach out and touch the subconscious impressions that drift around and within your consciousness. The rhythms and harmonies of music can help you do that: once again it's yet another way of getting your Inner Mind to pay a different attention.

As you know, your Inner Mind is constantly checking up to insure that you're doing as okay as possible. Your autonomic nervous system goes about its business without any conscious thought. Your lungs have been operating all the time you were reading this passage and chances are—unless you've have a bronchial attack or have something else that interferes with your breathing—you were entirely unaware of the movements of the gentle bellows that have been keeping you alive.

Yet you were aware as you read this paragraph that, just about now, you probably took a deeper breath than usual. You were aware that you were breathing as the air flowed in and out of your lungs. And you'll continue to notice your breathing until such time as your attention is caught, either by the words on this page or when something else brings your attention to focus elsewhere.

So if you have some way to quietly play soothing music, your Inner Mind will respond and you'll be closer to a pure cosmic unconsciousness procedure. The radio would be fine provided the music is right—the average synchronicity practitioner is likely to frown on head-banging hard rock. What many people call *elevator music* might be acceptable, or any other lighter classical stuff that you enjoy. During any of these kind of sessions, keep clear of *heavy* music of all kinds: The 1812 overture may be very attention-grabbing with its thunderous cannon, but what you're trying to do here is to soothe your subconscious. And stirring up your conscious mind with rousing strains of brass and reeds is pretty pointless at this stage in the game.

Self-Hypnosis

Then there's the thought that you might enjoy and respond to hypnosis, provided the idea is acceptable to you.

No need to flip the Yellow Pages to look for a hypnotist—a gentle spot of self-hypnosis will do nicely in this context, and for most people it adds extra zip to the lattice of coincidence.

Have you ever tried hypnosis? If so, you realize that much of the stuff you've understood through *B* movies is a lot of poppycock. A whole bunch of erroneous beliefs exist around who and what a hypnotist is and does. Forget the intense gaze, the swinging pendulum, the tuxedo, and other showbiz trappings. They all fit into the myth that movie producers and, unfortunately, some stage hypnotists maintain as dark and dreadful secrets.

The legend says that The Great Hypnaldo (or whatever outrageous stage name he boasts) has only to announce a few murmured words, swing his pendulum over you and *zappo!* you're deep in a delusion where you'll bark like a dog, see a wild lion in front of you, take all your clothes off, and in some of the nastier movie productions, rob banks, murder your spouse and, if the script happens to require it, sell your soul to the devil—although in this inflationary day and age I'm uncertain what the going rate may be for a human soul.

I jest, of course, simply because all that malarkey about trances and being under the influence of the hypnotist is ultimately false.

More Alert

No way does a person "lose his or her will" when under hypnosis. In fact, quite the reverse happens: Anyone under hypnosis, whether hypnotized by a professional hypnotist or under self-hypnosis, is more alert and more sensitive than usual. And if anything happens that would disturb the subject, particularly morally, the subject snaps out of whatever mental state he or she is in and comes fully awake, often hopping mad!

Hypnotherapy is gaining ground rapidly, especially in the treatment of some diseases, but learning to hypnotize oneself also has definite positive effects, especially where relaxation is concerned. However, because it's such a vital skill to accomplish, you'll know much more about relaxation when you reach Chapter 6. Meantime, you can try self-hypnosis quite easily right now, without having to do anything more than settle down and read the next section of this chapter.

May Drop Asleep

Find your favorite chair. A recliner is fine, but your bed is less than ideal. It's better to sit rather than lie when attempting this exercise: If you choose to try it lying on your bed, you may drop asleep, which may be beneficial if you suffer from insomnia, but what we're looking for is merely to get the elements of hypnosis going.

Try the exercise when your world is as quiet as possible. Attempting self-hypnosis when someone else is playing the stereo or watching television makes it hard for you to get into the hypnosis mood. Wait until everyone's asleep or gone out before you try this the first time.

Oddly enough, once you get the hang of self-hypnosis, especially if you tie it in with deep relaxation, you'll be able to hypnotize yourself at any time in any place. But for the first few times, go easy on yourself and try it when no-one is around and you're reasonably sure you're going to be undisturbed for a while.

If you are disturbed when you're trying self-hypnosis—maybe you're just relaxing down and the phone rings—all you'll feel is a mild annoyance. Answer the phone, complete the communication, then relax again, and start from square one.

So you've chosen your chair or recliner.

1. Sit back and take a slow deep breath. In ... and out. Again: In ... and out.

2. Now look at the wall in front of you. Continue those deep breaths.

3. Move your eyes upwards, so that you're looking a bit higher than is comfortable.

4. Find a spot on the wall—perhaps a real spot or just an imaginary mark up there.

5. Keep looking at that spot, continue those deep breaths, and then say, either aloud or in your mind: "Relax. Unwind." Spread the syllables out as you breathe. Keep your eyes wide open as you do this.

6. As you feel your lungs expanding say "Re. . . lax." Then as you start exhaling say "Un . . . wind." Get into the swing of the "Relax, unwind" thought or voice message. Keep it up for several minutes.

7. If your eyes water, blink. Soon you'll feel it would be a good idea to close your eyes. While you're listening to your own "Relax, unwind" phrase, remind yourself that your eyes are feeling tired. In your mind, say, "My eyes are getting tired. My eyelids would like to close." So let them close, but keep up the chant of "Relax, unwind." If your eyes have yet to close, now's the time to close them gently.

You Did It!

You know what? You've just achieved the first stage of self-hypnosis!

Is that all there is? By no means. I said this was the *first* stage. Next thing to do is to reassure your conscious mind that even if you're into a state of self-hypnosis, you're totally aware of where you are and what's going on around you. Go ahead, say it in your mind: "I am totally aware of where I am and what's going on around me." Yeah, talking to yourself, even in your mind, seems pretty stupid. But believe you me, it works. Nuff said!

Important Last Phrase

Now you can make your relaxation deeper by slowly counting from ten down to one, aloud or silently, and at each number say (or think) "Relax, unwind." When you reach *one*, tell yourself: "I am now more relaxed than I was before."

That last phrase is important. Some hypnotic techniques assure you that you're at once totally relaxed. And if you're still uptight and vibrating like a violin string, guess who thinks he or she is to blame? Why *you* do! So use this more gentle idea that you are more relaxed than before. You may still be wound up like a bow-string, but somewhere in your body and mind, you can accept that you're just a smidgen more relaxed than you were before. Get the drift?

You can practice this at any convenient time, but I do mean convenient. No way should you work with this technique while you're driving a vehicle or doing something which needs close attention, like carving a roast.

After awhile you'll find you can drift into this fascinating state to order. How long may that take? It depends on your personal psychological set, how wound up you normally are and how motivated you are to try self-hypnosis.

Initially, it may take you about ten minutes to reach the desired relaxed state. Eventually, you can get deeply relaxed within seconds, and you can effectively abandon the mental "Relax-unwind" chant and merely talk yourself down from ten to one.

Is It Really Working?

When you're good at that, you can, if you wish, try more self-hypnotic exercises, but, before that, you'll inevitably start wondering if it's really working, or whether you're just faking it.

> *Listen Up!*
> It's unimportant whether this state is real or phony. The actions and mental paths you're working on will be quite sufficient.

Yes, if you're a doubting Thomas you can experiment with hypnotic effects.

Maybe you'd like to try this one. One facility of your subconscious can be to create a pain-relieving finger. It can work extraordinarily well once you get the knack of it.

1. Go through your relaxing process.

Then once you're as relaxed as you can be for the moment, point one finger of one hand. Either one.

2. Then place your finger on the top of the wrist of your other hand. Feel the finger touching your bare skin.

3. Hold that pose for a full minute and think about what you're doing. Really think about it: Feel the pressure of your finger, decide if your fingertip is getting warmer.

4. Stay relaxed and, with your eyes closed, announce to yourself: "This is a pain-relieving fingertip. After I have slowly counted from ten down to one, my finger will work like a local anesthetic when I put my fingertip on the source of any pain that I or anyone else has."

5. When you've got that phrase into your mind put your 'healing finger' on to the area of the pain, close your eyes and think, "Discomfort gone. Discomfort gone. Discomfort gone."

Sure, it's that *with practice* trip again. Some people will be able to do this hypnotic analgesic procedure on their first try. Most others will need to do it several times before their subconscious clicks into what it's supposed to be doing.

This technique will work with surprising efficacy for minor hurts such as a head, back, or toothache. But before you do this procedure, first tell your *patient* what you're going to try to accomplish and make sure he or she is comfortable with the idea. Only then should you touch the person. And recognize that when this technique works, it's temporary only. If the discomfort persists, the hurting person must check with a medical practitioner he or she trusts.

It's surprisingly easy to move into a light hypnotic state, but if you want to go more deeply into the subject, you might want to co-opt a professional hypnotist, so you can feel what it's like to be hypnotized. If you can arrange that, then ask your hypnotist to plant a post-hypnotic suggestion in your mind, so that whenever you want to, you can drift deliberately into a hypnotic trance. But as I say, this is less than obligatory; it's merely an experiment for you to try, if you're curious about exploring your own mind (and body, for that matter).

Eventually, your mind will respond so that by the time you reach six or five in the countdown, you've already become fully relaxed.

Once you've reached that desirable state, you'll find it much easier for you to visualize whatever is in your mental field to increase your synchronicity energy.

Speak Aloud

And one further thought about this chapter. Several times I've suggested you speak aloud to carry out certain techniques. I suggest you give it all you've got when you're speaking. No need to be tentative. Shouting it out is ideal—unless you discover that your neighbors or room mates are listening. That can put a decided damper on your technique, so the next best thing is to shout the words and phrases in your mind. Does that seem strange to you? It's a simple trick.

Pretend you're rehearsing what you're going to say next. Think about the phrase ,but wait before you even think it aloud. Then, pretend you're going to shout the phrase forcefully. Think about how you're going to do it. Close your eyes if you wish, and then repeat the phrase mentally, so it reverberates in your mind. Give it a try and you may be amazed. Once you get the hang of it, you can stop worrying whether your neighbors think you're a kook because you used to talk to yourself!

And now back to the tricks and treats that can help you keep temporary coincidences occurring on a regular basis. Turn the page to Chapter 4, where you can find out how to lend a hand with shaping your own future.

Step 3:

Learn to give yourself permission to change your life to whatever you desire.

Chapter 4

Cooperate
With Your Chosen Destiny

Sow an act, and you reap a habit.
Sow a habit, and you reap a character.
Sow a character, and you reap a destiny.

—Charles Reade,
The Cloister and the Hearth.

Well here we are, moving right along as they say. We've had a look at how you can change your path in life and how to remove inevitable obstacles. So how do you keep this positive energy going?

Easy. You cooperate with your destiny. In other words, allow randomness to do its work without hindrances. Sure, whatever you choose to do, synchronicity will bring up unusual flukes and coincidences that match to your chosen life pattern; all you have to do is to give destiny a free hand and things will work out quicker and even more satisfyingly.

What's happening there? Well, it depends on what you mean when you say that fate or destiny, or even Higher Powers, are creating your desired events. Certainly, something's going on, but whether it's blind fate or angelic energy is anybody's guess. It might be a good idea to just let things happen and sure enough, your new world will become better and better.

Lucky Breaks

First thing you can do to help meaningful chance on its merry way is to be ready to pick up on new opportunities. What does that mean? Simple: Keep your ears, eyes and ideas wide open at all times. The way synchronicity works, as you've already been told more than a couple of times, is for lucky breaks to come your way. So, all you have to do is to recognize those breaks. Simple as that.

A classic example involves Doris Foster from Dallas. She went the whole hog and actually created her own wheel of fortune. The TV show, starring Vanna White and Pat Sajak, has been known to be great leisure entertainment, but Ms. Foster needed more than that. She cut out a cardboard wheel and then glued photos of a car, two people making their wedding vows, an electronic keyboard, and a check for five thousand dollars to the wheel.

Ms. Foster's first lucky break happened within a few weeks, when she was able to come up with the money for a new car. Meantime, a traveling gospel choir had sung at her church and Ms. Foster had been very attracted by Shank Robinson, one of the singers. You guessed it—in due course, Doris became Mrs. Robinson and her new husband gave her an electronic keyboard as a wedding gift.

So the car, her marriage, and the keyboard made three of the four lucky breaks that had been around the corner. Within a few months,

Mrs. Robinson got her final lucky break. The phone rang in her new home and Doris was staggered to find that she'd won more than the five thousand dollars, which had been her lucky break target. She won exactly twice as much when she'd been the lucky winner in a national sweepstakes competition.

Quoting this account by Frances L. Kittrell, a magazine correspondent, Mrs. Robinson declares: "I knew I was going to win. If you just open your heart and believe in good things, they're bound to happen."

Mrs. Robinson's lucky breaks are pretty much like positive thinking. But others are true chances which come out of nowhere, provided you're keeping your eyes on things that seem related. Often though, you realize what's happening too late to do anything more about it except make a note of the coincidence. Be aware of these happenings, your fate will never be the same!

Example: You're strolling along the sidewalk thinking about nothing much in particular, when you glance down and happen to see a book of matches on the ground. Two things you can do now. The first may be to walk on, thinking (if you notice it at all), that a discarded book of matches is a pretty much nothing, and it's unlikely to offer you anything new or exciting. But what if there's a note someone has scribbled on the cover? Do you still throw it away, thinking it's trash and it's none of your business?

That's where you jump on the opportunity. The second thing you can do is to pick up the book of matches and turn it over to see if there's anything useful on or in it. There you go—a telephone number. So at the next pay phone (or on your cell), you spend a small sum to call that number.

You'll either make contact or you'll miss out on making a connection. Chances are it's a wrong number anyway, one that's been disconnected, or perhaps a computerized voice tells you how you can be given a good time and it will cost only forty bucks or something equally uninteresting. Unless the call is interesting to you, hang up.

Of course, if the connection sounds fruitful, stay on line and follow through. That's how synchronicity works. But whether you get involved in something fresh you'd been unaware of, or whether you decide to break the connection, one way or another, you'll have changed your destiny, if only a little bit. Taking time to pick up the phone will have slowed you down.

A New Chapter

Years later, you may find that, as you turned the corner, (by stopping to pick up the matches and thereby changing your timing) you literally bumped into an old friend you last met years earlier in Chicago. As you greeted each other, you opened up a new chapter of your life. Perhaps the old friend needed someone like you to run his new computer business, and later you took over the company, and became a multi-millionaire, eventually retiring to Hawaii.

If you had kept walking without slowing down to make that call regarding the book of matches, you'd have gone on your way, and your old friend and you would have missed each other. Result: Well, maybe it took you longer to retire and you had to go to the trouble of a divorce and a second marriage to enable your spouse to get an inheritance that set the pair of you up for life. Different strokes, perhaps.

The pattern or dynamic that we call luck will somehow put you on the track you wish, but if you're keeping a weather eye for new chances at all times, you'll indubitably hit your personal jackpot of life quicker.

Free-Wheeling Fate

Regarding this idea of giving destiny a free hand, you can consider that while you're bopping along your merry way, you may be hoping that Ms. or Mr. Right is going to meet you, and certainly fate can set up such a meeting between the pair of you. That's simple for a free-wheeling fate to handle. But if you choose to shut yourself in your room to be a couch potato and watch television during most of your waking hours, you're kind of obstructing the synchronicity energy.

Sure, your perfect partner may indeed come and kick your door down. You've heard that destiny moves in mysterious ways, and one way of finding a gorgeous stranger marching into your living room could be that the legal powers-that-be have decided to have a drug bust and one underling got the address wrong. From that error can begin a fascinating sequence of events that brings you to happiness. Sure, that sort of unlikely thing can happen, but by and large, it seems having an active interest in the matter seems to make a difference.

Listen Up!
The process of synchronicity operates best when you are moving around meeting people, things, and energies.

Help the Energy

So how can you make this happen more easily? Strange as it may seem, you can use your personal hunches to aid synchronicity. Oh, right! The last time you trusted a hunch, you backed the wrong horse and nearly had your car repossessed in the bargain. If that's your idea, just sit back a second or two.

Remember you've got these uncanny quirks of your own destiny in your corner now. Things are already starting to straighten out the twists and turns of your fate so that what you *thought* was impossible yesterday, is starting to become possible today, and will be a fact tomorrow. How come? Believe you me, your hunch links are already seeking ways and means for you to win as suggested.

If you like this illustration, you're starting to be psychic—but if that term rubs you the wrong way, how about suggesting that your intuitive talents are becoming more accurate? Meaning the same thing but using different words, you could say that your extra-sensory perception is emerging. And probably an even better way would be to say that your spiritual energy is firing on all eight cylinders.

New Things Are Happening

However you slice it, things are happening in your awareness that are new and unexpected.

How do you know? Take time to think about what's been going right since you seriously started to read and absorb the words in this book.

Agreed, much of what's been happening you've felt to be coincidence. Even turning the pages of this book in preference to taking a walk has set up new patterns of your life that will lead to unexpected events in your future.

In the past few days, it may have been pure chance that you decided to walk downtown instead of driving. Maybe it was coincidence that

had things happen—you'll only recognize how things improved in your life later when that particular set of circumstance has run its course. And by the time that bunch of chances has been used up, you're onto yet another new path that leads to ... where? Truly, the choice is yours. All you have to do is to allow your destiny to have a free hand, and keep your eyes open for changes.

But What is Destiny?

While we're talking about destiny, fate, luck, chance, accident, fortune, or whatever you like to call the things that happen to you, what is this thing called *destiny*?

Shakespeare's plays say things like, "There's a divinity that shapes our ends, rough-hew them how we may," which seems to suggest that he believes in a kind of plastic fate—you can chip away with your freewill, but when it comes to the crunch, the Ancient of Days has the last say. We could ponder for weeks and still find unsolved answers; it depends what your source of thinking is.

I came across an interesting thought the other day regarding the relativity of knowledge. It's yet another theory of philosophy that suggests it's impossible for us to know what anything really is, since the knowledge of things is conditional on the mind's purely subjective forms of relating to its outside world. Leastwise, that's what I understood it to mean—like the Beatles sang: "Nothing is real." But they also added, "There's nothing to get hung about." Which is probably right: And my last word on this thorny thought about what things are real or unreal, I leave to René Descartes who said around 1630: "Cogito, ergo sum," which means something like, "I think, therefore I am."

So philosophies are fine, but let's get into the practical meat of synchronicity as you read Chapter 5 which really starts things happening in your life.

 # Step 4:

Allow randomness to do its work without hindrances.

Chapter 5

Pretend
It's Already Happened

The future has already happened.

— Buster McLeod

Now here's another key idea for you to think about. You've considered what this book can do for you. Chapter 2 has offered you how to get rid of misfortune for good, Chapter 3 has helped you remove some major obstacles which inevitably get in your way, and Chapter 4 has suggested how you can cooperate with your chosen destiny. With all that neat stuff going on, the next thing to bend your head to is to pretend all these events have already happened.

Yes, that's what I said. All you have to do is pretend. And for some folk, even that can be a challenge. The dictionary says to pretend is, "To assume a false appearance, or to make believe, as in play." And that may be the answer for you: How about playing a mental game, so that you imagine something to be true—even if your logic says it's unlikely to be literally true.

Making Changes

Look, already you've gone along with the idea of bending your thinking in new ways, so that you've considered making changes in your life. You've even thought of letting go and allowing destiny to open up new paths of your existence.

So here's the next thing to reflect on. As I suggest, make believe that all this marvelous stuff we've been thinking about has already happened. Pretend that it has.

If you prefer the different word, call it *visualize*. That's probably a more accurate term if you're into semantics, but I use *pretend* rather than visualize because, although there are some people who genuinely have trouble visualizing, most anybody can, if they have a mind to it, pretend or sham or act a role or use a dodge, wile, excuse, bluff, feint, trick, or disguise to achieve their specific ends.

So where am I going with this thought? Well, first I'm going to reinforce this previous idea. Pretend the outcome you so positively desire has actually happened. Remember this is a pretend exercise.

And why should we pretend? Because as far as your subconscious mind is concerned, it's totally indifferent as to whether something is real or whether it's imaginary. Your subconscious mind works in concepts; it's only indirectly connected with your material world. So whatever picture your conscious mind brings up for your subconscious to look at will be accepted by your subconscious, whether the picture is a real item seen by your eyes, or an imaginary thing that's produced either by your imagination or by deliberately pretending something has happened. Your subconscious mind will look at the scene and accept it for what it seems to be.

That's both marvelous and disastrous: marvelous if you're creating things you desire, because once you produce those things they'll become reality in your material world, but less wonderful if your mental pictures about you and your world are downers. That's why motivational books get written: What you think and say will become real, so think negative, and your life will be full of pessimism and loss, while if you consistently think positive, you get the best end of the bargain—all the way from mental optimism to physical wealth. Add the concept of purposeful small—even large—miracles happening, and the world's your oyster.

And one of the pearls in this particular oyster is produced by learning how to put a picture in your mind.

If you're one of the 17% of people who can clearly picture a scene or object, you're ahead of the game. We'll be discussing that in more detail in Chapter 7. But whatever your *pretend* quotient is, the small task right now is to close your eyes and think of something. Say a yellow cab, one that's traveled far, has had rusty dings and scratches in its paint work over the years, and is probably drifting a thin, blue smoke from its tail-pipe as it shudders away up the road. Or if you dislike vehicles, take a crack at seeing an elephant with its flapping ears, ropey tail, huge feet, beady and intelligent eyes, and gray flexible trunk.

Okay, end of the exercise. Whether you actually saw a cab or a beast behind the eyes of your mind is unimportant. Something happened in your brain. And what that something is ties in firmly into the sharpening of your synchronicity talents. So accept whatever your mind sent to you, kind of rolling it around your mental chops, and store away the impression for later.

One thing to consider about this latest topic is how your mind tends to create any of the mentally visual stuff I've been talking about. Most human minds tend to lay emphasis on some senses more than others. While describing a puzzling event to someone, you might say, "Do you *see* what I'm getting at?" Alternatively, another person, describing a similar set-up, might say, "I *feel* this is exactly right." Perhaps a third person would use other words, such as, "I *hear* what you're saying."

Tasting and smelling tend to be less productive when it comes to descriptions: "Fishy or dubious, this deal's going to work," or "I'm ready to relish this arrangement!"

So while you're exploring your mind and making pretend pictures, try to use as many of your five senses as possible. Instead of just thinking, "That feels good," when you're visualizing something, add the necessary phrases so it becomes something like: "That *feels* fine to *see* and *hear* myself *savoring* what's in good *taste*." Somewhat lame, but the phrase gets to express all your senses except your sixth sense and that comes later. I'm pretty certain you can do better than that in this pretending workout.

The Next Stage

It's imperative for you to realize that we're just creating pretense right now, but as synchronistic energies swing further along into your future, you're going to receive whatever you wish for. Ready to start the next stage of this phenomenal trip?

Let's try something easy first. We mentally looked at a grungy cab just a while ago, so how about sprucing things up so you're considering a new car? Remember, this is pretend. The *how* of it is still a potential expectation rather than a true-life reality.

Just close your eyes and think, "I was asking for a new car. And here it is. That's real nice." With your eyes closed, put some feeling into this. Enjoy the idea of this new car. Think about the new-car *smell* of the interior. *Listen* to the coach-built click of one of the doors. *Feel* yourself slipping back behind the wheel, with the supple cushions touching your thighs. If you like, just so this is going to be a five-sense experience, you can put your tongue out and *taste* the air around you as you luxuriate inside your new vehicle. Then still with your eyes closed, think about *seeing* this car with its bright chrome and smooth paint work.

An Impression

Now open your eyes. Look ahead in whatever direction you wish. Just for a brief moment, after you've done this pretend exercise, you'll get an impression of being in the car you've been pretending. Matter of fact there's a chance when you open your eyes that you'll be looking at this new car. Surprise, surprise! I'm kidding you, of course. In very few cases will anybody who tries this simple exercise receive a new car instantly. Chance and chance alone will occasionally work instant lucky breaks, but usually it takes a little time for the ideas you're creating to become concrete and change from in-your-head mental to here-and-now physical.

An Anecdote

Here is one useful example of how synchronicity works. This event happened *way back when*. My partner and I and our children had moved from South Africa, where we'd been living for four years, back to England, our country of birth. After the wide open spaces of South Africa's high veldt, Britain seemed kind of overcrowded, and our itchy feet soon suggested there were pastures new to be explored.

Neither my partner nor I could decide where to go. We were doing the tourist trip around Trafalgar Square in London in the UK when fate stepped in, in a big way. I was still thinking about a name for it, but we already knew that cooperating with destiny would turn things the right way in a hurry.

We were sitting at one side of the square by the fountains, looking at the lions and Nelson's column, when my partner stabbed a finger at one of the brochures we'd picked up from a travel agent.

"Look, they're offering assisted passages to Australia," my significant other said. "And over on this page, Canada's offering the same thing."

Both looked interesting. Neither of us had been to either country. Responses from the family ranged from "Cool!" to "Can we go today?" But who knew where we'd end up or what would happen to us?

Decisions, decisions! Finally my spouse said, "Flip a coin—that'll make the decision easier." But before we did that I said, "So if it's heads, we go to Australia, and if it's tails we go to Canada."

"And if it lands on its edge we'll stay where we are," said my son.

"Smarty-pants," I said. But the coin duly failed to stay on edge, and within weeks, we had launched ourselves into a new country. Hello, Canada!

Further Spice

That was some forty years ago and blind fate is still raising the ante. If you wish, you can do the same sort of thing. Mind you, we've come a long way in those decades and we've learned a lot more. If we'd done it all again, my guess is we'd have added more synchronicity tips and wrinkles to smooth our way. That might have added further spice to our destinies, and possibly shipped us to totally different parts of the globe.

That's the joy of this juncture: All you have to do is pick up and run with the ball, whether it's greasy or you score a goal, you're heading for satisfaction and success. It never fails.

You recall, early in Chapter 2, I said "All you need to do ... is to think about it. Just that. Nothing more."

Tell you a secret: That's really all there is to synchronicity. Everything else in this book, all the tips and wrinkles, extra exercises, and the like are merely support services. It's a clear case of, "We'll start with Plan A, but if that happens to be invalid or temporarily challenging, we'll go to Plan B."

Bringing that thought into this metaphysical sphere, Plan A is the central idea of synchronicity energy, based on the single vital concept of bending your head to create your desires, while Plan B is the supplementary stuff which boosts the basic accord syndrome energy and helps you to improve your aim and get what you want in short order.

You'll find a multitude of stuff connected with Plan B, and every little helps. In Chapter 7 you get a spot of numerology, astrology, Tarot card reading and palmistry—and please don't knock it until you've tried it! Chapter 8 offers you personal proof that synchronicity really works, Chapter 9 discusses, among other things, metaphysical concepts such as psionic activity and knowing the future, while

Chapter 10 rounds out the book with final details on how to make this whole recipe work.

But I'm ahead of myself. Next here is Chapter 6 that helps you to do something truly essential: to relax physically. Turn the page and soak up this bit – it's crucial.

Step 5:

Learn to Put a Picture In Your Mind.

Chapter 6

Relax Physically and Mentally

Music alone with sudden charms can bind
The wand'ring sense, and calm the troubled mind.

— William Congreve
Hymn to Harmony

Remember how I keep plugging away at the thought that all you have to do is to make a picture in your mind, and then your destiny will do its best to make everything happen the way it should so that you get your rewards? That's very true and as I keep saying that perhaps you've latched onto this method and you've already found things happening in extraordinary ways.

If so, that's nice. Told you so. But what if your synchronicity benefits are more an anticipation rather than a reality? Well, it could be that your body and mind are holding things back a bit. If so, this chapter gives you the scoop on how to open up to the energies which are waiting to serve you.

Metaphysical Energy

This united harmony energy—some people call it the music of the spheres —can literally move mountains, yet it is infinitesimal in its material nature. No regular electric measuring device will wave its pointer up and down as synchronicity energy is operating, because it uses metaphysical energy rather than physical power. Certain instruments, known as radiesthesia machines, can detect this mystical energy, but unless you really want one, buying one of those gadgets is irrelevant.

The fact is, that no matter how sensitive your average electrical or electronic measuring device is, its needle is likely to stay firmly at zero when this cosmic energy is operating. Nevertheless you'll know its power is working because of what happens around you in the way of delightful happenings which you can call *lucky breaks* or coincidences if you wish. Whatever you call them, you're on the right path to seeing your every last wish fulfilled.

However, because this system is so minuscule in its physical capacity, you can help the power along if you'll do one thing—which is simple for some people and extremely challenging for others. That down-to-earth thing needed in part of this equation is to physically and mentally relax.

A Screeching Halt

Here's where a lot of people come to a screeching halt. Relaxing takes time. Sure, you can flop on your bed for two minutes and announce, "I'm relaxed." Maybe you are. Some people can do

that. But most of us, when we think we're relaxed, we're merely recognizing that we're less stressed than we were before we laid down and announced we were going to relax. Some of us are unsuccessful at relaxing even when we're sleeping. In Chapter 10, I'll go more deeply into related relaxation techniques that may need more work than just what's coming at you in this particular chapter.

Do I hear a groan of displeasure? "I really have a problem relaxing because I'm too busy, too tense, too all sorts of stressful things. If I relax maybe I'll miss something in my life."

Comes With the Territory

Sure you may miss something. A peptic ulcer, a heart attack, perhaps a stroke—all sorts of neat maladies can creep up on you if you're continually uptight. Like the old cliché says, it comes with the territory these days.

So how about considering a schedule where, just for a few minutes a day, you literally learn to relax? Yes, many people need to be shown how to relax; some folks literally need to be wound up the whole time.

Sure, you may know how to relax a bit. "I'm going to relax for an hour," you may say. So you break out the lawn chair or open up your favorite recliner. Once you lie back, swing your feet up, and close your eyes, you're starting to relax. That's definitely a *maybe*. Your body may be starting to go a bit less tense but how about your mind? Still going a mile-a-minute, I bet.

Often, the stresses of the day press hard on you. Then there are the usual interruptions that come whenever you try to relax. Maybe the telephone or your cell needs immediate attention. Sure, it might be a client... but it's probably Danny from down the street, who wants to tell you how his day's going. So you settle that bit of unfinished business and your spouse needs your help, probably in the basement where the washer seems to have gone on the fritz. Neither of the above? Then maybe you're startled out of your relaxation when one of your kids taps you on your shoulder and says, "Um? Like, can we talk?"

Is it going to be a confession about shop-lifting? Or is your teenage daughter unexpectedly pregnant? Hopefully it's nothing as earth-shaking as that, but any interruption tends to make you more stressed than ever.

A Good Start

So what's the answer? Well, the first thing to do is to stop worrying about relaxing. That's a good start. Then, take it easy on yourself. Your first thought when you're reading this section is liable to be for you to say, "Relaxing's very low on my personal totem pole, mostly because I find there's too much going on all the time in my life."

And why the big deal about relaxing, anyway? Well, the straight answer is that it works really, really well, and synchronicity will thank you for it.

Look at it this way: Using synchronicity makes links between your world in and about you and the metaphysical environment within your deepest mind level—your superconscious, collective unconscious—or more simply put, your Inner Mind.

Now, seeing that everything we know about this universe suggests it's made of energy that's kind of coagulated into shapes we can work with, your purposeful connection is possibly an electrical or electromagnetic flow, and when physical muscular tension gets in the way, some of the positive effects of meaningful coincidence can be temporarily obscured.

Try It This Way

So getting relaxed can be very valuable, and even if you're a diehard stressed-out person, you can relax if you try it this way. And this way is ultra-simple.

What you need to do is to accept initially that you are tense. You're stressed. No necessity to make a federal case of it. There's no deadline for relaxing. When it happens, it'll happen. And you'll feel the benefits.

The secret is to relax a tiny bit at a time. Forget about the texts that say, "Using this method, in three minutes you'll be as relaxed and limp as a wet dishrag." Try it that way and the average person spends so much time expecting the dishrag state to become prominent, that the end result is more stress than ever. "Maybe I'm doing it wrong and I'll never relax," can be your cry.

First things first. Apart from there being no *best-before* date for you to become relaxed, there's no special way for you to relax. You may be a proponent of yoga, Reiki, Tai Chi, *shiatsu* or any of the

dozens of techniques that produce relaxation. Maybe you've got a relaxation tape or even a video to listen to or watch. If you've tried any kind of those procedures, and they work for you, then by all means carry on using them.

But if you're finding your relaxation methods are less effective than you'd like, here's yet another way of trying them. You're right when you state there's nothing new under the sun. What I'm offering you next is an amalgam of several methods of relaxation which works for many people, even those who've said to me, "I'm always tight as a bow-string. For me, relaxing is for the birds. I stay tense even when I'm sound asleep."

A Double-Edged Meaning

So here we go with yet another way of helping you become as limp and slack as that proverbial wet dishrag. But before we start doing it, you may need to consider a semantic definition: Even the word *relax* has a double-edged meaning. Many people think that when you are relaxing that's merely the opposite of working.

Practicing a hobby or getting involved in a leisure amusement is what relaxation means to some folk. So what we're looking at here is relaxation in the sense of getting rid of tension in a particular manner, and the first step in this process, strangely enough, is to recognize what's going on around and within your physical body.

Some Muscles Need to be Tense

It's unnecessary to worry about the technique itself: Right now, wherever you are, whatever you're doing, think about your body. The idea here is for you to learn to relax, and in this sense, relaxation means the total absence of any muscular contraction other than the regular tensions that operate within your body to keep you going.

Naturally, the idea of totally relaxing your heart muscles is out of the question. That muscle is destined to pump your blood around and do the multiple tasks of your body so that you remain alive. Obviously, some of your muscles need to be tense as they go about their business. So what you need is to slacken all necessary areas of your body, allowing the important keeping-you-alive stuff to continue to do the vital things.

If you relax the muscles over which you have control, your internal muscles, like your heart, stomach, intestines and other internal organs will also relax themselves.

Do you have five minutes to spare today? Anytime, morning, noon, or night. But a regular routine would be useful. Some people try a spot of relaxation when they first wake in the morning. Other folk find time to unwind during their lunch hours. Many will take five minutes between television programs, although this technique can be worked with the boob-tube on, if necessary. Whatever schedule works for you, will also work for relaxing.

Get Yourself Comfortable

Best if you can lie flat on the floor, with a pillow supporting your tail bone or coccyx, an area of your spine which got that odd name from the Greek kokkyx, cuckoo, coming from a fancied resemblance to a cuckoo's bill. Go figure!

Anyway, get yourself comfortable horizontally. A recliner would also be fine, but it's best if you avoid using this relaxation method lying on your bed—that way you're liable to drift off to sleep, and that idea is not fine. But if you're going the whole hog with this relaxing stuff, you need to be reasonably alert at this time, so you can get the next exercise going.

So you're lying on your back. If you feel your neck is straining, slip a slim pillow under it first. Now close your eyes. Gently. No teeth-gritting effort here. Be restless if you like. Shift and fidget all you like. Open and close your eyes in a blink if you wish.

Uncross your legs if you've already crossed them. Put your hands on whatever you're lying on with your thumbs at least six inches away from your legs. Stay where you are for a minute or two, and think about what's going on. Guess what? You're starting to recognize the tensions that are in your own body right now.

Depending on how padded your floor is, you may be feeling totally uncomfortable by now. So while you're thinking about your body, whatever it's doing right this moment, take a deep, slow breath, feeling your lungs open and swell. Hold the breath for a moment. Is your chest trembling or twitching? If so, you've pushed too hard and taken in more breath than you need to. Breath out and try the inhale again, but this time stop the inhalation before you start

trembling. Now hold the breath for a couple of seconds, then exhale slowly until your lungs seem empty, hold the position for a couple of seconds, then start inhaling again. Keep this going for about a dozen in-and-outs.

No Need to be Precise

Notice I've mentioned the phrase "a couple of seconds" at the inhale and exhale positions. No need to be precise about how long you hold the breath. Some relaxing techniques tie the timing to your pulse rate, so that you inhale, hold your breath for two or three heart beats, exhale for up to six heart beats, then keep the lungs empty for another two or three heart beats. That works well for some people: Personally, I like to try and keep this technique as simple as possible. Finding your pulse and then counting the flub-dubs of your heart is okay if you know how, but for some folks the whole process can be frustrating, making you less relaxed, rather than more.

Now you can stop your heavy breathing routine and drop back into your normal habit of breathing. Still flat on your back, shrug your shoulders two or three times. Now shrug one shoulder, moving it up and down. Then shrug the other one, and relax back.

Next, turn your head and neck to the right as far as you can without obvious straining. Do the same to your left, then bring your head back to center again. Do that left-and-right move, to and fro, four or five times.

Less and Less

While you're doing all this, pay attention to your body. Notice where you are feeling creaks and stresses. You'll find as you practice this technique, that the minor—maybe major—creaks and groans get less and less every time you do this relaxation workout.

Having worked on your head, you can carry out a brief session throughout the rest of your body. Lift your hands, lace your fingers together, and place your hands on your solar plexus, just above your navel. Inhale normally and feel your stomach respond, allowing your fingers to move with the inhalation. Then, as you exhale, push your palms onto your body, quite firmly, so that you push an extra bit of breath out of your lungs. Do that three or four times, and then put your hands back to your sides again.

Next, raise your right knee up to your chest, and reach up to clasp your hands just below your knee, pulling your leg as close to your chest as you can. Hold that pose for about twenty seconds, then unclasp your hands and return them back to your sides. Unfold your knee and rest your leg back onto whatever support you're lying on.

Repeat the process with your left knee.

Now wave both feet around for about twenty seconds, moving them in small circles. Then put your feet on the floor again.

And that's it. You're okay after that, are you? Well, reasonably so, although that knee stuff might be a chore now and again.

Also Relax Your Mind

That's one way of teaching your body to relax. But naturally, this being a holistic thing, along with relaxing your body, comes relaxing your mind. That can be another story entirely, yet it's no harder to get your mind to relax than it is to get your muscles to unwind. It just takes thinking about. Although there are many different levels of your mind and soul operating simultaneously, for the sake of simplicity, we can consider your mind as being at three distinct levels.

Up front, there's your conscious mind. That's the part of your brain which is the guide and, hopefully, the captain of your ship of life. At this level of your mind, you manage logic and reasoning, you set up goals, and also somewhere at that level you find and store memories.

Your Engine Room

Next you can consider your subconscious mind as the engine room of your ship of life. Your subconscious holds a storehouse of experience. It's got a vast amount of knowledge—yet it has no true reasoning power. There's information in plenty, but it's locked away if it's unacceptable to your conscious mind. In fact, even when subconscious stuff gets to the surface of your mind, the thoughts are usually disguised suitably for the conscious mind to accept. It's very probable that your subconscious can recall all that has ever happened to you, from—or even before—your birth up to the present time.

But whatever is happening at the various levels of your mind, sleep opens the doors to your subconscious and seemingly your superconscious as well.

And your superconscious—sometimes known as the collective unconscious—is an even more enigmatic place. You can think of it as being deep below your subconscious, but that kind of situational concept is only a tiny part of the beginning of the story. The superconscious in some sense is everywhere. It's certainly part of your mind, probably part of your soul, if that's acceptable to you, and from a metaphysical point of view, your superconscious is all-knowing and close to omnipotent.

Filtered or Censored

Certainly from the superconscious comes material that is rarely available to your conscious mind, and even then, if the information does reach your conscious mind, the data will have been filtered or censored by your subconscious. Some mystics say that *All Knowledge* is in your superconscious somewhere, and it knows the past, present, and future, as if time is an illusion—which it may well be, if some of the philosophers such as René Descartes or Nicolas Malebranche are correct in their musings.

But *retournons à nos moutons*, a peculiar French phrase that says literally, "Let us return to our sheep" and means "let's get back to the subject," which is, of course, relaxation and its benefits.

Whenever any muscle of your body is tense, even briefly, your brain records the sensation. The tense muscle sends messages through your nerves to your brain.

Why does it do that? Because the brain is interested in what's going on, where your body is in your particular space and time, and probably why the muscle is tense in the first place. And to get that information to your brain, your nerves relay messages from muscle to brain resembling wires in a telephone network, but in a much more digital manner. As those messages are being transmitted, electricity shoots back and forth from the muscle to your brain.

Now we know that when an electric current moves from one place to another, the wires (or nerves, rather) radiate electromagnetic pulses that can be detected with the right apparatus. Those pulses, especially if the muscle is very tense, can be relatively large. At the same time, your intuitive energies are also moving around your body and mind. And if the nerve energy overpowers the intuitive energy, guess what? Your intuition goes for a loop!

Exotic Hardware

Conversely, your body is constantly being flooded both internally and externally with electromagnetic fields of types that were only ideas on the drawing-board a few years ago. Nowadays, cell phones, microwave towers and ovens, television, space satellites, atomic piles, radioactive elements, and even more exotic hardware spray electromagnetic fields at and through you. Your nerves (or better your axons and neurons) respond to these energies: Any time a conductor (like your nerve cells) is hit by an electromagnetic field, whether that's ordinary magnetism or the electro type, your nerves get a tiny surge of energy known as eddy currents. Those random flashes of energy affect the clear paths from your axons or neurons, and what started out to be a clear message from your body to your brain, can end up mildly scrambled. That's fairly okay—I guess it's mildly deficient, but acceptable when your brain is using relatively gross energies to work with. It's when you get down to your Inner Mind that things start going less accurately.

But what can you do? No way can you easily be wrapped up with copper gauze to keep the radiation away. It would work, partly, but having a copper suit complete with helmet, boots, and gloves a bit like an astronaut would be uncomfortable to say the least.

So what's the answer? I guess one fair answer would be: *If you're unable to beat 'em, maybe you should join 'em.* In other words, you've inevitably got a mess of electromagnetism affecting your brain, mind, and soul, so all you can do in effect is to shout louder!

Swamps Your Mind

What I'm trying to say is that, these days, you have major cacophonies of radiation affecting you, and they can swamp your Inner Mind and similar areas. Your Inner Mind's attempts to bring useful messages up to your consciousness have been snowed under by man-made static and other radiations. It's a bit like you being in a quiet room, knowing that next door someone has cranked a stereo up to full thud-thud base boost. If you try to tell someone in the stereo room some information, just an ordinary voice is a waste of time. You'd have to get the message across by making an equal noise of your own.

That's what you can do with the total harmony that reaches your very soul. The outside world is a noisy place at almost all frequency bands, but when you get good at radiating your own signals via cosmic randomness you'll be able to cut the racket down to size by metaphorically building a loud-hailer.

I'm using metaphors here, but the objective is the same. Yes, you can make contact with metaphysical energies, but nowadays, it's getting to be more and more of a challenge.

So, good luck in that particular area, and you can help things along by turning to Chapter 7 where you can check what kind of tools destiny has given you to reach your chosen goals.

Step 6:

Know Your Territory.

Chapter 7

What Has Destiny Given You to Work With?

There are two things to aim at in life:
first, to get what you want;
and, after that, to enjoy it.

— Logan Pearsall Smith
Afterthoughts

Coming along well. You've read about changing your life path and removing obstacles in the way, and you're already cooperating with your chosen destiny, so that cosmic chances can bring your desires into wonderful reality.

An intriguing episode in Robert A. Monroe's book, *Journeys out of the Body*, shows how intentional premonitions can work.

Monroe relates a classic synchronicity incident. It seems that during his teen years, Monroe had been looking forward to a particular get-together one Saturday, but unfortunately his finances couldn't cover the necessary two dollars admission fee. His parents couldn't help, and when he went to bed on the Friday night, he still hadn't found any solution to his problem. Sadly, he figured the party would have to go by the board.

He awoke on Saturday morning, and, suddenly, had a clear belief that the crucial two dollars was under an old board leaning on the ground alongside his house. At breakfast, he was still mulling over his depressing money problems, and more to put it out of his mind rather than any other idea, he went outdoors where the board was lying. It was covered with mud and leaves, and, in fact, there was no obvious way that anyone would turn this mucky board over and abandon a couple of dollars. Nevertheless, Monroe checked, if only to set his mind at rest.

Monroe pulled up the board and was amazed to find where the board had lain were two folded, dry one-dollar bills.

End of problem—no doubt picayune in some respects, but exactly what Monroe needed, and that's precisely how it works—think positively about what may happen, and intuitive energy brings home the bacon.

Obviously, Monroe had a strong need to bring a lucky break, and it would probably be to your advantage, if you yourself tried the visualizing exercises, so that you've pretended your outcome so strongly, it has a reality of its own. Metaphysically speaking, by putting this picture before you, it's already happened somewhere in the planes of time and space which we have still to fathom. But just because time and space are still enigmas, it's perfectly okay to see the results right before your very eyes, even though nobody can actually say precisely how this process works.

But work it does, and while you're experimenting with the words in Chapter 6 about relaxing, you might look further ahead and wonder if there's anything more you can do to keep the metaphysical pot a-boiling, to increase your chances of getting where you're going even more efficiently and quickly.

In these previous chapters, you set everything going, and if you want to quit while you're ahead, by me that's fine. The energies will continue to work and you'll see your chosen desires coming into being. In fact, some of them may have happened already.

Still in Your Future?

So what if you're a slow starter? You've done all the work so far, yet your first synchronicity project is still in your future.

Did you do something wrong? Uh-huh! You did nothing wrong, but maybe something else is slowing things up a little. That something is, for want of a better word, your personal destiny. And we could go off on a cloud of philosophy and theory if we tried to decide exactly what the word *destiny* means to you. Call it your fate, fortune, appointed lot, or kismet. Or you could think of your destiny as part and parcel of what you were born with.

Your Logic Capacity

First point to consider is a mental thing. Over the years of your life so far, how much logic and reality have you learned? Are you a person who likes to call a spade a spade, or do you abandon material logic now and again and weave personal fantasies? Reason why I'm asking is because in this fascinating world of cosmic consciousness working, sometimes things happen which seem to be totally illogical as you head towards a goal. In Chapters 3 and 4 you were invited to think about a goal and then cooperate with fate or destiny and see that you reached whatever goal you'd created in your mind.

On Welfare

Typically, I remember a guy called Kevin who knew me and my sometimes bizarre ideas. I think it was more to say "toldja so!" when it wouldn't work, rather than Kevin's thought that he might use and benefit from synchronicity—but greatly daring, he aimed to get himself a car.

At the time, he was on welfare, and getting a vehicle, licensing it, paying the insurance, and putting a spot of gas in the tank was well into cloud cuckoo land. More than a trifle disbelieving, Kevin tried setting up purposeful energy. What could I lose?" he said.

Two weeks later he was due to come to my home in Montreal, Canada, with a bunch of friends. He was running behind schedule, but when he finally arrived he said, "Sorry I'm late, guys, but I had trouble parking my car."

I figured maybe he'd been doing some heavy visualization and was just pretending he'd bought the car. But no, Kevin was telling the truth. He made us walk to the end of the block to see his new vehicle, and knowing that two weeks earlier he certainly had no car and seemed to have no way to buy one, we thought maybe he'd stolen the wheels.

"Do you mind?" Kevin said tersely. "No, I own it. And if you guys will listen, I'll tell you how it happened. Last week, I got a call from my older sister, Linda. She and her fat cat fiancé, James, had decided they'd go to Sydney, Australia, and maybe get married there. Linda asked me if I'd do her a big favor. 'Only if it's free of charge,' I said, knowing I had less than two buttons to rub together."

"My problem is my car," said Linda. "You know, my yellow Mustang? I'm really not interested in shipping my wheels all the way from here to Australia. James already has his Jag, so I think starting with us having two cars down under would be a waste of money. Maybe after we're married we can do the two-car thing. And after that, who knows? But I wonder if you'd be a real sweetie and look after my Mustang until after we get settled in Australia? I'll pay the insurance and licensing and all that, and I'll even throw in six months servicing and gasoline."

A More Amazing Event

The deal was struck and a truly astonished Kevin got the use of a nearly new Mustang, and within a short while, an even more amazing event occurred.

"Linda called me from Sydney," he said. "They got married as planned. And when she discovered her pa-in-law had given her an SUV as a wedding gift, she said freighting the Mustang all the way across the world would be less than a good idea, so she said I could keep the Mustang with her love."

See what I'm getting at? Destiny (or *something*) allowed Kevin to get his car, despite it being a fairly illogical event. If you'd been in the same boat, would you have expected Kevin to get his car, despite the odds against his success? And yes, almost at the same time he got a job, a new partner, and another residence. That was a few years ago, and I've since moved far away, but I still get an occasional e-mail from Kevin, telling me how well he's doing. Quite a change from Kevin's original forlorn hope and the bounty he now enjoys.

Cause and Effect

"It's remarkable how it happened," he said recently to me. "Really there should have been no way for me to get that car and the rest of the stuff. Looking back at what went on, all I had to do was to sit back and let the future take care of itself. I suppose there was a cause and an effect going on, but if I'd stayed with straight common sense, I'd probably still be with the *same old same old.*"

Certainly, becoming too coldly logical about the process can hold things back for you.

Try a small experiment, if you will. By the time you've tried this and have seen it work, or alternatively discover it's pretty unproductive, you'll personally be able to understand if your personal logical set holds you back from fully using synchronicity or whether you're ready to move into the method like a duck to water.

This takes just a couple of minutes and the only gizmo you need is your hand and your nose.

The Double-Nose Test

Ready? Open your hand—the one you write with is best—and cross your middle finger over your ring finger. If you've got plump fingers that may be a bit of a challenge, but try it anyway.

You'll probably need to push the two fingers around a bit, using your other hand, and if this hurts, just quit. It's an interesting little trick but whether you apply it, or instead, decide it's a waste of time, it's hardly of vital importance to your synchronicity process. But once you've twisted those two fingers as suggested, turn your hand over so you're looking at the palm. I'll go with the majority here: What I'm describing is for a right-handed person. (If you're left-handed, transpose the phrases about right and left side of the nose to left and right side).

Lift your hand with the two bent fingers up towards your nose. Careful: Take it slow, and gently rub those two fingers up and down the outside of the tip of your nose. If you peek at what you're doing, you'll find you've got your ring finger touching the right side of your

nose and your second (or middle) finger touching the left side of your nose. Now, close your eyes as you stroke those two fingers.

The Vital Effect

How does it feel? Does it feel peculiar? Unusual? As you stroke gently, can you feel two noses touching your fingers? That's the vital effect. Many people instantly recognize that they've apparently got two noses touching their face. Does that happen to you? If so, synchronicity working will be a breeze for you.

But what if, no matter how much you rub your nose, you firmly say something like, "It feels strange, fiddling with my nose, but so far as I can sense, I've just got one nose, like I've always had."

If that happens, stay cool. Most likely, you're a strictly rational person who goes by the book, someone who logically knows that two plus two equals four all the time. Good on ya, sport—we need more people like you in this age of illogic. So if your nose says it's merely singular and refuses to split into duality, be happy! Yes, maybe it may take you a little while longer to create your synchronicity stuff but once you're there, you'll know that it was truly logical from start to finish.

So how about you folks who went, "Crazy! I can feel two noses as true as true. What now?"

As I said earlier, if you accept that phenomenon, you're ahead of the game. Because of the way your mind operates, you're able to hang on to an illogical idea: You know you've only got one nose, yet it feels as if you've got two noses. In the area of psi-sense that's ideal, because frequently you'll get a similar sensation when you're working to make things happen. You'll be using random chance to create something special for yourself, even though logically you'll know it's unlikely to happen. That's what occurred with Kevin in the earlier example. So enjoy the two-nose sensation because you'll know you're moving in the right direction.

Tactile Illusion

As a matter of interest, why does this twisting and bending produce the odd effect? It's a sheer tactile illusion. Your finger has been moved to a position alien to its usual place. If you just touch two fingers without them being twisted, you'll surely feel your regular single nose. It's the twist that does it, nothing more.

Okay, so you've tried that small test. Want something more? Here's something you can find out about yourself that can help you with this work, and this time, all you need is a pencil and paper or a calculator.

Your Destiny Number

In the metaphysical area, there's a system known as Numerology (and if you already know about it, my apologies — you can skip the next bit). Numerologists will also despise me, because it's hardly the simple science I may make it appear here. So for all you numerologists, please forgive the simplicity—I'm merely making a point. Numerology states that almost anything you can experience or describe can be turned into the numbers from 1 to 9.

For instance, if your name is Wendy, by simple substitution, the number of your name is 8. How come? The most widely held style of Western numerology takes the numbers 1 to 9 and matches them to the letters of the alphabet from A to Z. So you end up with:

1	2	3	4	5	6	7	8	9
A	B	C	D	E	F	G	H	I
J	K	L	M	N	O	P	Q	R
S	T	U	V	W	X	Y	Z	

This little table is all you need for this exercise. We were checking the name WENDY. Under the letter W is the number 5. Under E is also 5. Under N is (you guessed it) 5 again. Under D is 4 and under Y is 7. So add those numbers: 5 plus 5 plus 5 plus 4 plus 7 equals 26. Add the 2 and 6 to make a single figure so 2 plus 6 equals 8. Wendy's name number is 8. Sure, there's much more—for instance if a name number is more than 9, as Wendy's name is, you keep going until the product is a single number. When you come to a zero you can ignore it. (There's much more about 11 or 22 or 33 and several other arcane numbers but this is enough for here and now).

You'd really need to read a whole separate book about the intriguing subject of numerology, and no doubt you'll find several in most libraries. As I said before, I'm being simplistic, but for the purpose of this text, all you need to know is that as you're working these simple examples.

An Inherent Ability

So what can you do with Numerology, as far as working random chances is concerned? Once again you can decide if you have an inherent ability to work these wonders or whether you're one of the folk who'll have to work a bit harder than others to get this regime going.

It all comes down to your birthdate as far as this next smidgen of numerological lore is concerned. There's a particular number known as your Destiny Number and you find that figure just as simply as you showed yourself what a name number is.

To find your Destiny Number note down your birthdate in numbers alone. For instance, if your birthday happens to be August 15, 1972, first turn that month into a number: January is 1, February is 2 and so on to December being 12.

Now write your date of birth on a piece of paper. That example of August 15, 1972 comes out as 8, 15, 1972. Now just as you added the numbers with the name number, add the figures of your birthdate. Example is 8 plus 15 plus 1972. That adds up to 1995. Now add those figures as before: 1 plus 9 plus 9 plus 5 equals 24. Add those two figures together and the answer is 6.

Anyone who was born on August 15, 1972 has a Destiny Number of 6. That little doohickey works for anyone who knows his or her birth date—and it's simply done by reducing the birth date to a single digit as we just found.

And what does that mean in the real world? Numerologically speaking it shows you your life motivation, what you should do to make the most of yourself. By noticing what this number signifies you are supposed to live up to its energies. Once again it's a 1-to-9 path we're looking at.

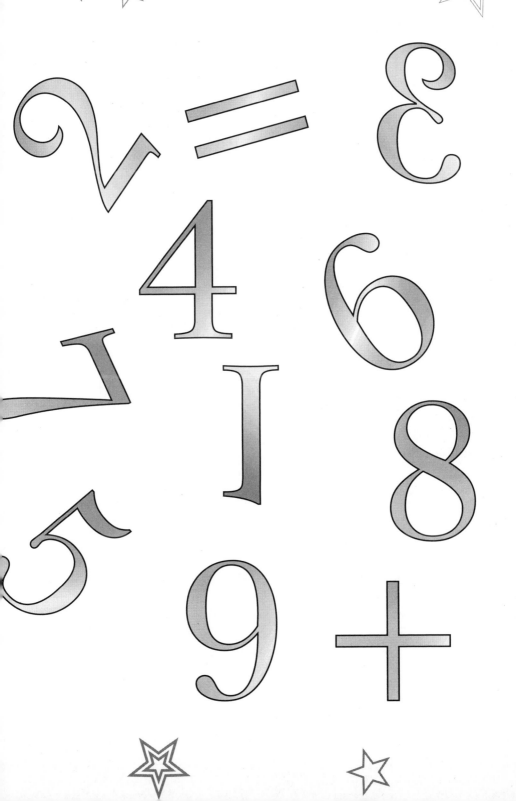

If your Destiny Number is 1, you're a loner, someone whose path leads to solo success. You tend to be the responsible person at all times, and you should always be looking for ground-breaking ideas and new techniques. Take pleasure in rarely taking the tried-and-true path: You're a true pioneer, especially in commerce and finance. Being a leader is your true heritage.

If your Destiny Number is 2, you lean towards finding the middle ground whenever matters of stress or pressure come up for grabs. Your strength is in teamwork and you'll be equally adept at supervising staff, family, or partners. Be the diplomat at all times and your destiny will also include useful compromise, and it can lead you to harmonious triumph.

If your Destiny Number is 3, you're a classic communicator, maybe a writer or an artist, with a need to seek out answers, and to bring a spark of difference to your affairs. You're certainly talented in many ways, and as early as you can, you should assess those abilities and go for the gusto. Your strong self-expression will bring you recognition and wealth.

 **If your Destiny Number is 4,** you are a builder. You positively enjoy routine operations which can become worthwhile, long-term enterprises that grow both materially and financially. The fruits of your work can last for centuries, producing literal structures or economic security for you and your descendants.

 **If your Destiny Number is 5,** you've always been known to do the unexpected. You're restless and rarely stay in one place for long. Capitalize on this by traveling, note your splendid sales ability and look for ventures that are experimental and need your special touch to make them work perfectly.

 **If your Destiny Number is 6,** you're a sociable person who has the talent to teach. You also have a marked facility to persuade others using reason rather than force, while your inborn enthusiasm and your concept of comfort will inevitably bring you to that hard to pin down item named happiness.

If your Destiny Number is 7, you tend to be an introvert who seeks his or her own path in life, frequently leaning towards a mystic approach, possibly with interests in reincarnation. Researching hidden truths, either as a detective or a counselor, will strengthen your spiritual point of view.

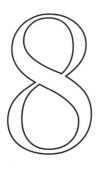

If your Destiny Number is 8, you should think big. This number is reckoned to be the path of the executive, a significant stimulus to acquire riches and deal with money. Business and commerce are your forte, with a marked aptitude for managerial skills, efficiency, and aggressive personal success.

If your Destiny Number is 9, you're a person who knows how to bring any project to a grand conclusion, to dump anything which is over and done with, and to move on to greater heights. You crave freedom and liberty and you'll seek for it always especially when you get involved in metaphysical thinking.

Your Specific Purpose

So now that you've decided what your Destiny Number is, you can decide how it fits into the way of events making a fortuitous result. As you set up your specific purpose, recognize what Destiny Number goes with your objectives.

If you're a 1, you should aim for single-handed goals. You and you alone will find these things work best for you—no crowd scenes necessary!

If you're a 2, you'll get your most startling results when you have a partner involved. Learn the techniques together and you can double your pleasure.

If you're a 3, you'll find your most satisfying effects in a creative milieu. No matter what your project is, the best outcome will be if you apply your evident clarity of mind.

If you're a 4, you'll enjoy creating material objectives, ones that have visible outcomes that last for ages. You'll be especially good at anything connected with construction.

If you're a 5, your forte is to change things. Whatever your purpose is, make sure that the result is something that radically alters the *status quo*.

If you're a 6, you'll find your optimum purpose will be to change any disturbing situations. Look around, think what needs to be done to restore harmony, and with a little concentration, it's done.

If you're a 7, you'll bring your best creative results when you work in secret, and you're a person who'll get amazing results simply because your destiny leans you towards magical undertakings.

If you're an 8, you can go for the largest projects you wish, especially if your goals involve money. Your number is the one that helps to bring wealth your way in buckets.

If you're a 9, you should look toward projects that have yet to be investigated. Think of a most unlikely event, set it in motion and then be astonished at the result.

Remember, what we're looking at in this section is whatever will help you get your objectives created most efficiently, accurately, and quickly. So even if you're a 1, for instance, you'll inevitably have to go it alone. You'll find it easier if you do, but if you choose to get involved in a group of fortuitous people, you'll discover you're like cream: You'll automatically come to the top. Similarly, your Destiny Number may be a 5, yet you're desperate to be like a person whose Destiny Number is 4. So your destiny goal of changing things (5) needs to be altered so you have more of your material nature (4) coming into your free will picture. That's reasonably effortless: All you have to do is work at it a little harder than you would have to if you were working with your own Destiny Number. Get the picture?

Astrology Is Useful

The next element that can help you on your way is the science-art of the Sun, Moon, and planets. Carl Sagan once said that Sun Sign astrology is an obscure form of sexism and discrimination—we slot people into one of twelve categories without taking into account their individuality.

That, as they say, is maybe: Despite Sagan's system of belief, other authorities suggest that accurate astrology shows your uniqueness, rather than your similarity to others. Chart the Sun and Moon and eight planets in the wheel (forget the asteroids which are now firmly part of the astrological practice. And also the new planet which has just been discovered orbiting further out than chill Pluto) and there are more than 340,605,000,000 ways of splitting up the wheel of the zodiac, and each one is different. That's scarcely categorizing; that's individualizing in a big way.

But without getting into the complications of a complete horoscope, here we can get useful inputs by considering a totally basic horoscope where the astrology chart is divided into twelve segments identified as the familiar Sun Signs. Despite Mr. Sagan's slightly acid comments, depending on what their Sun sign is, some people will find it easier and others a bit more challenging to create their synchronicity projects.

Four Groups

The horoscope is divided up in four groups of signs that represent the four elements of Fire, Earth, Air, and Water. The Fire signs are Aries, Leo, and Sagittarius. The Earth signs are Capricorn, Taurus, and Virgo. The Air signs are Aquarius, Gemini, and Libra. And the Water signs are Cancer, Pisces, and Scorpio.

If you're a Water sign, you're in luck: You folks are more intuitive and sensitive than most and you're also the leaders when it comes to effortless plan of chance working.

At the other end of the scale are the Earth signs. You tend to be the most logical people of the horoscope and if you've read the earlier part of this chapter, and know about the "two-nose" maneuver, you'll realize that sometimes logic can get in the way of the operation of invisible energy working. That's okay: But you may find you have to work somewhat harder than average to bring your objectives to completion. One thing's for sure—once you've fixed your goals in your sights, you Earth sign folk will hit your targets and maintain the results.

Such solid decisiveness may only on occasion be true for either Air or Fire signs. Their projects will prove to be easier to create than Earth signs and less easy than Water signs. What the Air signs need to recognize is that they can all too easily be distracted from the business in hand. Having set up an objective, an Air sign person may find something more interesting to do and forget that some projects may need tending a little so that destiny can do its wonderful work.

Fire signs can have their own dilemmas: If you're a Fire sign, notice how forceful you can be, which is fine when you're inviting undertakings to come to fruition, but poor when you realize how stubborn you are. In your case, it's likely to be a question of letting destiny do its work without too much prompting: Your style of dynamism can hold back your proposed venture simply because you've decided that's what should be done and steadfastly stick to your guns.

Moon Phase

But whatever your Sun sign, you can add to your simple astrological lore by finding out what phase the Moon was in when you were born.

That's going to take some flicking through that bunch of figures and symbols called an ephemeris, but you might be able to co-opt your friendly astrologer to give you the information.

Broadly speaking, every twenty-eight days or so, your personal life goes easier. You've never become aware of that phenomenon? So check it out this way. When the Moon slips into the same phase as it was in when you were born, things go better and synchronicity becomes more energetic.

If you were born on a New Moon, then whenever that slim silver crescent peeks over the horizon, you're likely to get more successful in your plans. Similarly, if you were born at Full Moon, you can see better outdoors at that time (if the weather is bright and clear) and you're also a person who is more likely to hit his or her targets at that time every month. And if you happen to have been born sometime between the Full and New Moon, you'll need to do a spot of minor mathematical calculation. Offer that tame astrologer a couple of bucks to give you the answer. After all, even spooks need to eat.

Biorhythms Can Also Help

Another minor assist along your path to recognizing blind chance with Lady Luck can come from Biorhythms, the art-science of charting cycles of your life.

The theory of the discipline holds that there are three energy cycles that operate in your body and mind. Those cycles were recognized by a German doctor, Wilhelm Fliess, when he was exploring the onset of contagious diseases. His statistics developed with other medical people, such as Viennese physiologist Dr. Hermann Swoboda and Dr. Hans Schlipper M.D., when he speculated that the human body runs on regular life cycles of 23, 28, and 33 days. The shortest cycle, having a duration of 23 days, they labeled the physical cycle; the longest biorhythmic cycle which runs for 33 days, they called the intellectual cycle; and the cycle in between, which is 28 days long, they named the emotional cycle.

The Day You Were Born

Actually charting your biorhythms starts from calculating how many days have elapsed from the day you were born up to the present time. Once you have your date of birth you can chart the swings of the three biorhythmic cycles and establish at any particular day which of your cycles are ascending or descending. Your physical cycle charts your energy and staying power; your emotional cycle monitors your positivity and confidence; and your intellectual cycle maps when your mental responses are most agile and your creativity is highest.

With those cycles, the theorists propose what have been called *critical days,* and those days identify when you are likely to be indecisive or vulnerable.

Intellect Swings

As far as synchronicity is concerned, the most significant sequence is the 33-day cycle, the one where your intellect swings regularly from high to low and back again. If you can plot the ups and downs, you'll find that on a particular day you reach a peak of creativity and intuitive perception and then about 16 or 17 days later, you reach your bottom limit where your intuition is less accurate. And, of course, about another 16 days later, you're back to your peak again. Finding those peaks will indicate when your awareness is greatest, adding extra force to your primal energy.

To calculate the crests of your biorhythm waves takes a fair bit of math. Certainly, you'll need your calculator. You'll also have to decide when you intend to discover your peaks and valleys. Being on a 33-day cycle, the peaks are inconsistent with any regular rhythm such as monthly or weekly.

Get your calculator handy and I'll take you through the steps. First is the *when* of it. Once you can set up one of your biorhythm intellectual peaks, you'll know that every 33 days onward you'll hit another peak. And naturally, halfway between each peak is a low that says, at those times, you're less aware than usual.

Times Will Vary

Now recognize what we're going to look at here is approximate; the times will vary a couple of days either way from exact. Nevertheless, you'll hit the right peaks close enough to be valuable.

So here we go into yet another unknown area. What's your most recent birthday? How many leap years have elapsed since you were born?

So write down how many years you've lived from birth to this recent birthday. Divide the answer by 4 and then get rid of any fractional figures that may be on the right side of the decimal point. Make a note of this whole number first answer. Let's call that answer LY (for leap years).

Now multiply your current age in years by 365. When you've got that answer call it CA (for current age).

Now add LY to CA. That figure represents how many days you've lived so far—at least, up until your latest birthday. Call that DL (for days lived). Divide that last figure (DL) by 33 and note the solution. Call it BC (biorhythmic cycles). That figure represents how many biorhythmic cycles have gone by since you were born.

Now here's the tricky bit: check your calculator. Almost certainly, the figures will show a whole number, a decimal point and a bunch of other numbers to the right of the point. Subtract that whole number from the solution you've just found. Now you'll see just the period and numbers on the right. Multiply the answer by 33. You'll have an answer which is less than 33, once again with some figures on the right side of the decimal point. Forget those fractional bits: the whole number represents where you are in your first biorhythm cycle after your birthday. You can call that your IS (intuitive swing).

UP SIDE OF YOUR CYCLE

If Your IS is 8 or Less

If you get really fortunate you may find your IS will be 8 or less, and if that's so, you're moving on the up side of your cycle. To reach your first intuitive peak after your current birthday, subtract your IS number from 8. Whatever that answer is, you're on top of an intellectual peak. Note the day on your calendar then use your calculator to mark your peaks every 33 days for the rest of the year—or the next year and so on.

If your IS is Between 9 and 33

Okay, so what if you're one of the 75% of other folks whose IS comes between 9 and 33? It's a similar trip: to reach your intellectual peak which was just before your IS, subtract your IS from 25. Whatever that answer is represents the top of one of your intellectual peaks. Then, just as we calculated in the previous paragraph, note the day on your calendar and mark your peaks every 33 days into the future.

Here's an example to show you precisely what you need to know during your intellectual cycle, which is the one that works best when your biorhythm cycles are highest.

Example: James Doe, our guinea pig, is forty-six years old. How many leap years has he lived so far? Divide by 4 to know that answer—and forget any fractions—whole numbers only throughout this exercise. So, Doe has 11 leap years, and for the mathematically minder, we can call that LY (for leap years). Next, multiply Doe's current age by 365 and that will be 365 x 46 = 16,790, so call that CA (current age).

Now, add LY to CA and that figure represents how many days he's lived so far and you can call that DL (days lived); for this example, it's 16,801. Now, divide that figure (DL) by 33 and note the answer—call it BC for biorhrythmic cycles. This answer is 1,509, and you can diaregard any figures on the right of this calculation Next divide 33 from this latest calculation. Then divide 33 from this latest calculation and Mr. Doe's answer is 15. So Mr. Doe is right on target for his intellectual swing of about 16.

Mr. Doe should watch for any synchronistic events for the next two or three days for he needs to be wary—he can run into what are known as critical days, and he can either leap through to a peak or swing downwards until his next IS.

Several Books

And that's it. If you're further interested in the subject, a whole slew of books have been published on Biorhythms, and if they're still in print, George S. Thommen's *Is This Your Day?* or Henry Sill's *Of Time, Tides and Inner Clocks* would interest you.

Of course, there's plenty of software around which will quickly chart your biorhythms.

This is, of course, yet another off-shoot of such contingent causality which will help you in your task of hitting your personal best on a regular basis.

Your Hand Has Answers For You

The final section of this metaphysical-style chapter concerns palmistry. That's correct—by looking at your hand, you can see whether you're an intuitive individual.

There are a couple of areas of your palm that will help you make your decisions. One is on your palm on the side below your pinkie. For this simple set of tests, you should look at which hand you use to sign checks or contracts with. Put that hand under the table and look at the other one.

Have a good look at the palm of this hand—you're going to be studying it for a few minutes. Now, pick up the hand you put under the table, point your finger and touch the top of your pinkie of the other palm. Slowly stroke your finger down toward your wrist. Stop your finger about an inch before you're about to slide your finger off your palm and on to your wrist.

Where you're poking your finger right now is known as the Mount of the Moon (or Mount of Luna). Palmists know that this area shows what's going on in your intuitive or spiritual area. Around this area do you see a lot of lines or creases on the palm or is your hand as smooth as the proverbial baby's butt?

No Lines?

If you have no lines, or almost none, in that area of your palm, you're likely to be a pretty obstinate person who is fixed in your ways. No problem—you'll do well with that psychological set, and I'd be the last person to try and alter your way of thinking. I have to say, though, that you may need to loosen up a little before your ultimate outcome procedures can give their full energy to your life. Learn to relax those shoulders, turn your lips up instead of down and think about anything that really made you laugh last year. That may be all you need to click lucky chances into high gear.

The converse to the smooth Mount of Luna is the palm that has a multitude of creases and lines on that mount. That indicates a highly organized sense of subconscious and intuitive energy. As well as having regular dreams at night, you've got an innate sixth sense for this psi-related stuff. Congratulations.

And as a side issue, when you're looking at this hand, notice if you have two intersecting lines running about an inch from the edge of the Mount of Luna, forming a V, pointing diagonally towards the pad of your forefinger. If you have that metaphysical sign, you're distinctly psychic and that will help causal happenings no end.

Your Thumb

The other feature to look for is your thumb. Raise it like a hitch-hiker, then swing your whole fist until your thumb is vertical and you're looking at the knuckle or nail of your thumb. Now, run your eye down from your knuckle down to the base of your thumb. What shape is it? Is your thumb quite plump, so that it looks like a small barrel between the two knuckles? Or is your thumb kind of waisted, so that as you look at it, the knuckles are larger than the central piece? Or are you halfway there, neither plump nor thin but kind of straight up and down so that if you lay a pencil beside your thumb from knuckle to knuckle there's no daylight between the pencil and the thumb?

If you have a waisted thumb, you're the person who is most likely to make undetectable fortune ventures happen quickly. The *barrel* thumb is the most challenging for such efforts; a thumb like that suggests you'll have to work harder than average to get your objectives flowing. And of course the in-between thumb is just like it says: benefits will come somewhere in between easy and challenging.

Astrological and Palmistry Assessment

If we weigh up the above suggestions, the person who is a Capricorn (an earth sign), who has a bare Mount of Luna, and is a true skeptic in the way of intuitions will probably have to work pretty hard to get the chance energy to work. While on the other hand a Cancer with lots of lines on the Mount of Luna, and who has a waisted thumb, is likely to be already creating startling objectives as soon as the technique is described to him or her.

The Imaginary Block Test

Another consideration, after you've looked at your biorhythms, your astrology data, and your palm, is that you can start a new assignment by deciding how clearly you can visualize an imaginary event. 'Way back in the 30s, a Dr. Grey Walter did some interesting work on the human brain. During his research, he discovered (hardly surprisingly) that human brains have marked variations. One particular aspect of the brain is significant to our personal application of synchronicity, and that's the visualizing ability.

Dr. Walter discovered that one in five people hardly visualize at all. In other words, such a person when told, "Close your eyes and then think of a green Volkswagen" will *see* nothing except the inside of his or her eyelids. At the other end of the scale, Dr. Walter found that about the same percentage of people when asked to try the same test could produce solid three-dimensional pictures of the car. And, typically, some 60% of people when asked to *see* a green car were able to get strong feelings or mental pictures of part of the car, like the glass of the windshield or the black rubber of the tires.

The upshot of this experiment of seeing in your mind's eye is that the more clearly you can visualize, the more easily you'll be able to work with your latent spiritual energies.

Your Personal Visualizing Ability

For the fun of it, try this assessment of your personal visualizing ability. Read this next section slowly, thinking about what goes on in your head as you become aware of the words. It's probably a good idea to absorb this bit—skipping this section and reading it later might spoil the fun —there's a mild kicker in the tail of this segment, which will be absent after you've experienced it the first time. In other words next time you read this section, unless you've totally forgotten what it's all about, the surprise end point I plugged into the narrative will be gone.

So here, at least the first time you read it, is a visualizing analysis that will tell you something more about how your mind works.

As you read these words, stop at the end of each sentence, close your eyes and be aware of what your brain is telling you. After you've thought about the experience for a few seconds, open your eyes and read the next sentence. Continue doing that until you've absorbed the whole section.

Ready with this new awareness bit? So here we go!

A Small Wood Saw

Pretend, or see in your mind's eye, that you're holding a small wood saw in your hand. You choose which hand: You're going to be using the saw in a moment so make sure you hold the saw with your stronger hand. With your other hand, imagine you're holding a child's wooden block, about three inches on a side; you can feel the weight of the block as you hold it, with all five fingers around the block.

Now pretend you've braced the wooden block against something solid; a table, a bench, maybe a wall. Move your thumb away from the block and swing your other hand across so you're ready to start sawing the block in half. Start sawing, and as you do that in your own time, think about the smell of the wood as you're cutting the block. Hear the sound of the saw as you move it backward and forward. Even though you've closed your eyes, watch how the saw blade is now deep into the wood. You're still cutting away, backward and forward, and almost suddenly you finish the cut and half of the block drops on to the ground with a thump.

A Couple of Questions

That's the end of the visualizing exercise. Now, before the concept drifts away into memory, here are a couple of questions:

a) Did you, in your mind's eye, actually see what you were doing?

b) As you cut the block in two, did you see sawdust falling?

c) During the exercise, were you worried you might cut your fingers?

d) If you did cut yourself, did you feel any pain?

e) Did you actually hear the half-block fall to the ground when you finished the cut?

f) What color was the block?

g) During the visualization, what happened after you had finished sawing the block in half?

The answers to these seven questions will flesh out your awareness of this whole metaphysical technique and will show you what kind of level your visualizing power is at.

Multiple Choices

Give the first five questions (a) through (e) multiple choice answers, with your responses rated from 1 through 5 as:

1. Definitely no;
2. Possibly no;
3. Could be either way;
4. Possibly yes;
5. Definitely yes.

For the sixth question (f),
rate your answer from 1 through 5 as before:

1. I failed to see the block altogether;
2. I missed noticing any color at all;
3. Maybe I saw a sort of color but it was only a fleeting glimpse;
4. I definitely saw a color, it was red (or blue or whatever);
5. I saw a vividly colored block with several primary colors mixed together.

For the seventh question (g)
also rate your answers from 1 through 5 as:

1. Zilch happened; I saw nothing like a block;
2. I saw myself looking at the block and wondering what I should do next;
3. I put the saw away and swept up the sawdust;
4. I looked around the room and figured there must be some way I could use two broken halves of the block;
5. I sawed up some more blocks because I realized I could make a new board game from the half-blocks. I took on a partner and promoted and marketed the game and we made a million dollars together.

What Might Have Happened

Of course, those answers to the seventh question are wide open to consideration, and your choices would no doubt be different; what I'm trying to express is merely the idea of what might have happened.

Now, having rated yourself through all seven questions (a) through (g), what was your total?

5 (or less): As I mentioned earlier in this chapter, you're a remarkably logical person and you may be an accountant, a mathematician, a computer programmer, or a scientist. When it comes to using synchronicity energies, you'll probably have to work at it longer than most other people, but once you get the hang of it, the technique will never leave you.

Between 6 to 15: You've got the basis of these metaphysical skills well within your mental grasp. Practice making mind pictures of anything, anytime, and you'll move to the top of the class in relatively short order. Probably you'll be someone who starts with small projects and graduates to the really significant ones. (See Chapter 8 if you have any problems about this skill range)

Between 16 to 25: Congratulations! You're a natural for these intuitive projects. Just keep doing what you're doing the way this book recommends and your results will continue to expand and flourish.

Between 26 to 35: Careful here! These happenings can become almost too good to be true. What you have built into your mind and soul is a kind of overstatement procedure that can, because of the way you've been designed, have you become more than a mite too enthusiastic in your effects. Learn to be very specific with your project goals and stipulate limits of how much, how long and how often!

Interesting Areas of Intuition

Okay, are we still moving right along? Because here comes a thought-provoking section which ties a blue ribbon on the synchronicity technique. You could say one of the more motivating contacts is finding and using intuition to practice your new-found talents. And you can gain further progress by using symbolic cards to get specific answers in your life.

Do I hear the do-do-*do*-do theme for the *Twilight Zone,* or the background music behind Leonard Nimoy's baritone voice in his show *In Search Of,* or have those shows finally gone to those Great Television Ratings in the sky? Both those shows, probably still on your TV screens in rerun after rerun, explore the unexplained. One of the more intriguing things that such enigmas look at, for instance, is why it's possible for a bunch of colored pasteboards to produce intelligent answers when looked at in a particular way.

I'm referring of course to the Tarot cards. Why the Tarot cards *work* is mystifying, but work they do, and while you're honing your cards which will make sure you get a royal flush, you'll find that using the cards will help to put a keener edge on the influences that shape your life.

Seventy-Eight Mystifying Cards

Once again we have a check mark here: Is the Tarot for you? These seventy-eight cards are either fragrant or malodorous of arcane power, depending on your opinions and beliefs. Some people are actually scared of what are, after all, simply a set of playing cards created long ago. Certainly back in the Middle Ages the Tarot was esteemed by some people and quite the reverse by others. The abhorrence crew were chiefly dyed-in-the-wool, though possibly mistaken, devout people who saw the cards as heretical: Certainly, even today some individuals refer to the Tarot cards as the *Devil's pasteboards*.

Be that as it may, the pictures and colors of the deck carry a peculiar fascination, and many people, seers, fortune-tellers, and mystics alike, use the Tarot cards to their personal benefit. As you can, should you wish to explore yet another small but valuable byway of synchronicity energy.

This may seem to be some kind of a break from orthodox motivational routines. Perhaps it is, but using the Tarot cards has definite useful side effects during your search for meaning and value in this experiment.

New Objectives

Here we can look at what the cards are, what they do, and what you can achieve with them. In the process, you'll achieve several new objectives, all of which can help you to find more harmonious ways of navigating into the unseen, uncharted, and sometimes scary future.

Primarily, you'll be learning a method of reading the pictures and symbols on a deck of cards, to give you answers to questions which can be deduced neither by logic nor known facts. Sure, you could call that fortune-telling if you wish, but the Tarot goes far more than that, and on the way, you'll be using deep levels of your mind which usually remain in the background of your conscious thinking. Just as a muscle benefits from gentle exercise and eventually becomes strong and healthy, so the use of the Tarot cards seems to teach your Inner Mind to do the equivalent of sit-ups and knees-bends, so that it increases in strength. You can, therefore, easily tap the vast storehouse of knowledge and experience which exists in the Inner Mind. In brief, the study and use of the Tarot can allow valuable thoughts, impressions, and intuitions to float to the surface of your mind as you learn and interpret the whys and wherefores of synchronicity.

The Legends of the Tarot Deck

A great deal of the Tarot's story is shrouded in allegory, the mists of time, and a bunch of fascinating stories that may be literally true—although you should be suspicious of some of the more fanciful tales, especially when they're printed in the tabloids.

The story of the Tarot is in some ways a chronicle of yesteryear and also a tale of man, myth, and magic. Virtually all studies begin by declaring that nobody really knows where and when this mystic deck of cards came from. That's a decidedly challenging concept because it's tricky to sort the legends from the truth.

We do know that some Tarot cards were hand-painted in Italy around 1400 AD, and although nobody's sure of the dates, there are

ancient decks in the London British Museum and in the Pierpont Library in New York City. Yale University has another deck and so has the Cincinnati Art Museum.

Previous to that century, the whole picture is murky: Some speculative types think the Tarot was the invention of a dude named Thoth, the Egyptian god of knowledge and understanding. Apart from Thoth's antecedents, even the name of the Tarot itself is obscure, although there's usually a smidgen of fact, even with the most outrageous myths.

For instance, one tale goes far back in time when a gang of high priests decided they were going to write a book with all the knowledge of the universe in it.

That labor of love took about 2,000 years to get the data out—there were apparently no computers at that time. Nevertheless, at long last, the book was ready to be printed.

I guess Bobby Burns said it well: *the best laid schemes o' mice an' men gang aft a-gley.* Sure enough, when the king of ancient Egypt, the Pharaoh himself, found out about this encyclopedia mission he was somewhat incensed.

"These characters seem to have stolen a march on us," said the Pharaoh, "and a lot more than that, what I'm really ticked off about the deal is that they haven't offered me a piece of the action."

"Should we wipe 'em out?" the Chief Vizier said.

"No problem," the Pharaoh said. "Just burn their stupid book and then tell everybody it never existed."

Of course, the priests were *ESP* experts, so they knew what the Pharaoh was doing.

"We'd better hide our book," the High Priest said, "or else, far in their future, some folks will never find out the hidden knowledge of the cosmos."

The High Priest thought for a moment.

"Listen you guys," he said. "Here's what we're gonna do. We'll make this an illustrated work and put the secrets on cards. Then I'll run a bunch of copies of the cards and you're going to go out into the wilderness and give these cards to anyone who wants them."

"So," one doubting Thomas said, "who's going to look at these cards? Secrets of the universe or not, most of these losers will burn the cards for kindling as soon as winter sets in."

"So let them know that these are gaming cards," said the High Priest. "Show them a few betting games, and since most everyone loves to wager, those cards will be valued chattels. Before long, clever individuals will understand the secret ideas of the deck and become skilled at things like soothsaying and psychic work."

The Cards Are Still With Us

So the priests started to hand out the cards and they've stood the test of time.

First the gypsies (Egyptians) declared only they could understand the Tarot cards.

But sitting in the wings were many mystics who also wanted to get noticed. For instance, Madame Helena Blavatsky, who was born in 1831, writes that the real originals of the Tarot are hidden in giant metal urns which were buried about a hundred centuries in the past somewhere in Europe.

On the other hand, a different Tarot tale suggests that when Alexandria was destroyed with its books and libraries, the scholars from all over the globe met in Morocco and made Fez the hub of mystical skills. The problem was the language barrier—everybody spoke their own lingo—so the scholars made a kind of secret pictorial code which anyone with a modicum of intelligence could recognize—hence the Tarot, 78 cards, with four suits of 14 cards each called the Minor Arcana, and 22 more spiritual cards separate from the suits, called the Major Arcana.

Relations Between Earth and Heaven

Whatever their starting place, the Tarot's curious and picturesque cards form a coded exchange of ideas demonstrating the relations between earth and heaven. The artwork acts as an input for the mind's eye and everyone translates the pictures in their own particular manner.

Changing the Originals

Of course, very soon, know-it-all folks went ahead altering the initial designs, and long before the millennium, there were more than two hundred assorted Tarot decks in print, simply because everybody had (and still has) different ideas of what the Tarot is.

Basically, first viewing the four suits, they're directly linked with four areas of existence. Various Tarot buffs suggest the Pentacles are serfs, the Wands are merchants, Swords designate the upper class and Cups indicate clerics.

Another pattern, using material, emotional, intellectual and spiritual points of view, suggest the four suits show associations.

And whatever areas we look at, regardless of the changing ways of seeing the Tarot, four suits are always the foundation of the deck.

For instance, Pentacles symbolize things you can see, feel, touch, taste or smell—the material things of life. Pentacles often talk about money, real estate, belongings, and security.

Wands are also materially connected but they have some mental adjuncts. They refer to problems to be solved, plans to be examined or challenged, perhaps attitudes to you or your environment that need looking at.

Swords are much more emotional and mentally linked. They speak of desires; essential judgments; emotions of pleasure, anguish, tenderness, illness, fitness; foes and associates, expeditions, helps, and hindrances. They're very busy with their symbolism, are those Swords, and they're often two-faced.

Cups are very mental cards, sometimes leaning toward fleeting connections, though more often tied into spiritual themes. Love, of course, close friendships, abilities and skills, especially creativity, new enterprises, the seven deadly sins and peace and prosperity are all Cups-oriented subjects.

Modern Decks

Over the years the Tarot has altered, and when the cards came into common use, they promptly became branded the *Devil's Pasteboards*, since many of the cards had religious drawings on them.

One of the Popes got totally fixated about one individual image, the one entitled *The Tower*, as he believed it symbolized the abolition of the church. One thing led to another, and pretty soon, the holy establishment proclaimed that the Major Arcana cards would be ritually destroyed by fire to terminate these sacrilegious items once and for all. When that virtuous inferno cooled, all the cards were altered to make them much more bland and seemingly less pagan. Even the four suits were changed: Pentacles changed into Diamonds; Cups turned into Hearts; Swords became Spades; and Wands were converted to Clubs.

Whatever the facts of this matter, these *new* decks of cards shrank down to 56, as the 22 major arcana cards were expelled in disgrace by the church. So that left King, Queen, Jack, and Page, then 10 down to ace. But worse was to come: The female Page (sitting between the Jack and the 10) became known as The Virgin, and once again the lofty principals of the Church dumped the four court ladies forthwith. So there went another four cards into purgatory or even purdah, bringing them down to the accepted deck of 52 cards that we know in the present day as standard playing cards.

Count the Cards

The Tarot has witnessed a tough road from Egypt, where it may have been started, through to the present day. But despite its trials and tribulations, the Tarot is flourishing very well. Regardless of the moral oppressors who threw out the old Tarot cards, next time you unwrap a new deck of cards for your poker game, try counting the cards. Only 52, right? Wrong—you'll find in your new deck of Bicycles there are at least 53 cards. One of them, grinning at you notwithstanding all that has been done to get rid of him, is *The Joker, The Fool* of the Tarot deck.

Fable? Myth? Fact or fiction? That's truly irrelevant: What is crucial is that the Tarot is a way to penetrate the confidential data of the cosmos, and by extension, open up to your own destiny like a flower being watered. If you're prepared to open your psyche with this vital side trip, you'll love it.

Even before we glance at ways of performing a Tarot card reading, we could speculate how they work, for explaining a spread of the cards by a Tarot expert can be a somewhat astounding, sometimes even mystical, event.

Cards on the Table

Methods vary from reader to reader, but the outcome is that the reader shuffles the cards, puts some of them on the table, and then goes ahead and tells a whole bunch of neat stuff about your past, present, and future.

And there comes the enigma. If the reader can see something coming in your future, can you avoid it, especially if it's some kind of

calamity? Sure you can, unless you happen to have gotten together with one of what I call the GAD (gloom and doom) readers.

A GAD is part of the down side of Tarot reading. Such a person will tell you that you're "under an evil star" or maybe "you've got someone who's throwing black magic at you." Whatever, your GAD will almost invariably insist you leave mucho dinero on the table before you leave, otherwise (the GAD says) you'll continue to have bad luck, and even worse things will happen to you—try the latest urban legend and prepare to meet thy gloom!

I suggest you keep a country mile (at least) from such scam merchants.

Recognize also that a reading is flexible. Carving a reading in immutable granite is unwise. If something the reader says must happen to you, quite frankly he or she is wrong. Any kind of reading should merely suggest things coming your way so that you can use your freewill to accept or reject the events.

A Union Between Minds

What the cards seem to do is to provide a union between your conscious and subconscious minds, and the Tarot symbols open some kind of a gate that allows contact to information that's usually protected in the depths of your mind. Knowledge of the Tarot enables you to view a set of colored pictures and decode them into a narrative that has meaning and usefulness to you.

Sure you can do that. You've been doing similar mind tricks ever since you started to read. Look: NET. What do those three letters say? "Net," okay? A fishing net, maybe a tennis net, a woven, open fabric perhaps to keep birds off your strawberry patch.

Hold it, though: Those letters were never actually saying anything. The were just marks on paper, and when you look at the word *NET*, you're viewing about nine short, straight lines, four vertical, another four horizontal and one diagonal, making up the letters *N*, *E* and *T*.

It's your mind that turns those shapes into a word. Sometime, probably when you were at a school, you caught the knack of looking at marks and lines on paper or on a blackboard to make words, and, later, sentences.

The Tarot works in a similar way, but instead of lines and marks, you look at colored pictures. With some practice, you discover that the shapes in front of you can be read, just as you're reading this page. But instead of single words being strung together into sentences, the pictures produce whole narratives that tie into existing conditions or even foretell the future.

Many Stories

So what do those colored images denote? Good question. The Tarot tells a story—many stories, actually. In one way of looking at it, they tell the whole chronicle of Homo Sapiens—provided you can recognize it. In symbols, they spell out conditions of being, both vices and virtues, and ways to discover peace, happiness, and paths to harmony.

Now, the *How* of It

So all I've written about the Tarot so far is the *what* of it, rather than the *how* of it.

As I said earlier, you can buy yourself a book about Tarot reading, absorb it, and probably later rather than earlier, discover you're an excellent Tarot reader. Or you may have gotten bored with the whole episode and decided there are more interesting things to do than look at a bunch of attractive pictures.

But assuming you've begged, borrowed, or otherwise gotten hold of a deck of Tarot cards, upcoming is a simple yet deep method of using the cards for your personal benefit.

Certainly we're in yet more uncharted territory where the only correct path is the one that feels right for you. No one but you and your Inner Mind can find the way to the successful conclusion of any Tarot reading, but if you would like to cut loose from applying *book* meanings to the cards you'll respond to conscious and subconscious clues from the pictures. Want to give it a try?

When you first look at a Tarot card, at the outset ask yourself what is happening in the picture. Then accept all answers, however off-the-wall they may seem to be. And as you take a look at this method, keep asking a simple question as you look at the cards: "What does this mean to me at this time?"

A Basic Tarot Spread

There are almost as many ways of running a Tarot spread (some people call it a "throw") as there are Tarot readers. There's one traditional *throw* known as the Celtic Spread that uses just ten cards, and that works very well for many readers. Then there's the whole-pack spread known as *Etteilla's Throw* and that can take hours—it uses all 78 cards, and it also uses them four times!

But for the moment, what say we just look at an ultra-simple spread? You may be relieved to know it uses just four cards. And by the magic of the Tarot you'll find just as convincing answers from this mini-spread as you can get from the multi-card throws.

Prompts

When you're looking at any spread, any written notes, definitions from books, or what I call *hint* words, are just prompts for your mind to latch on to. Listen to and speak out any thought that appears in your mind, no matter how odd. But do try to keep any mental narrative non-threatening, especially if you happen to be reading for a friend. And always remember, the Tarot and the universe has at least two sides: optimistic and pessimistic, white and black, blissful and miserable, bright and murky, strong and weak. And so on. And when you get into the cards you'll discover both the constructive and the destructive energies that swing around the Tarot.

Whatever transpires, be sure that when you've finished, you should end the narrative on an *up* or positive note. But before we move into an actual reading, recognize that no matter what any experts say, there are no set rules in the Tarot, merely traditions.

Ready? So shuffle the cards. Anyhow you like. If you're a fumbler, so fumble! Just mix up the cards of the deck until it feels right. What do I mean by that? Everything or nothing. Just mix the cards around until you think you've done it enough. I used to do quite a bit of Tarot reading and one of my favorite clients was a person who was an arthritis sufferer. She and I used to have great fun when I would carefully put the deck of cards on her frail hands then with a *one-two-three!* she would throw the whole deck up in the air. It was then my job to pick up the scattered cards, square up the deck and then start the reading. It worked like gang-busters!

Deal the First Card

So when you're ready, deal the first card face up on the table. Imagine a clock face: Put that first card at the 9 o'clock position. Then deal a second card face up, and put it on the 6 o'clock position. Deal a third card at 3 o'clock. And a fourth and last card at the noon position. That's the end of the throw: Next comes the reading.

Relax a bit—Chapter 6 tells you how to do that, but for the moment just sit back and look at the four cards you've selected. Try to clear out all judgments of your surroundings or the state of the world. Let new ideas float up in your mind, kind of feel for a new level of meaning growing in your mind. Speak your thoughts, whether it's to a person who's listening or to a tape recorder you've switched on.

Colors First

Start with the 9 o'clock card, the one you put down first. Look at the foremost color of the card.

If it's **yellow**, especially in the sky as a background, the start of that reading suggests optimism, expansion, and control, while if the yellow is on the ground or in the forefront of the picture, safety and security is foretold.

Blue, with a sky background suggests victory, harmony, and agreement, although if the blue is chiefly water, that points to healing energy.

Red: If it's largely on clothing, the start of the reading says you're dealing with a stubborn person who is physically energetic.

Green leaves show growth, while green clothing also indicates healing. Green grass will prompt you to see progress and stability.

Orange is interesting. If it's in the foreground, expect boredom, although with minor advancement. An orange background to the card designates orthodoxy and stubborn concepts, probably like a parent. Orange clothing shows secrets and the need for privacy.

Purple is neat: you're given the impression of great spirituality, so look for intangible benefits; material ones are less likely when this color turns up.

A **gray** sky background says energy is low—maybe that's yours! Any change will take much effort and it might be a good idea to start with a fresh slate. Now if it's a gray foreground you should take time to relax and think. And gray clouds show doubt and uncertainty.

A **black** background looks like depression or the unknown.

Now the Symbols

We're just looking at the first card, remember? You've looked at the color, so now check the symbols. I've indicated a few and arranged them alphabetically.

Bird: shows minor irritation.

Cover: (like a serving dish) asks "What's hidden?"

Cup: shows spiritual and emotional involvement.

Dog: (which you may see as a pet or even as a beast) brings your carnal nature to the foreground.

Drapes: another "what's hidden" symbol.

Fish: shows information, possibly gossip.

Fruit: agreement, growth, maybe pregnancy.

Heart: strong emotions.

Hill: a challenge.

House: security.

Moon: subconscious decisions.

Pair of pillars: gateway to a new phase of life.

Pentacle: money and possessions.

Pyramid: old knowledge.

Rock: an obstacle.

Snake: an enemy or more gossip.

Snow: coldness or lack of something important.

Square: permanence and strength.

Sun: new beginnings and advancement.

Sword: your objective is at hand, provided the sword has a point to it. If the sword point is hidden, or there's more than one sword on the card, you must decide your priorities.

Throne: recognition, authority, and a position of power.

Tower: protection.

Wand: your personal plans need deciding.

Waves: pressures and challenges.

Wheel: expansion.

Wreath: victory.

So that's the first card examined. Next cast your eyes on the second card, which is the 6 o'clock position. Apply the same colors and *hint* words. Say anything you like, but keep it reasonably short.

Next look at the third card at the 3 o'clock position. Again check the color and *hint* words. And finally, gaze gently at the noon position card, the fourth one. Same trip: Think about the colors, then the hints.

Almost done. How do you feel about this little spread? Did you get any emotional reactions? What's the general atmosphere of the spread: calm, dull, turmoiled, materialistic, happy? Finally, when you've thought about the four positions look again at the noon position card. That, traditionally, is known as the *peak* position. Whatever train of thought comes to mind, those are your clues to your future.

As an example, I shuffled my own trusty Tarot deck and set up a four card spread just to see what happened. Using only the hints and colors mentioned above, here's what I found.

My 9 o'clock card has red clothing, and checking the symbols I certainly see a hill—a mountain, more like—and a kind of throne.

My second card, at the 6 o'clock position, has a blue sky background, and a few green leaves sprouting out of a wand. There's also a kind of throne nearby, although it's mostly covered by a yellow cloth, and a person in red sits on the throne.

Card number three, at the 3 o'clock position, has a gray sky background with more green leaves, while the symbols include a sun.

And finally card number four, the *peak* position. The background sky and the foreground are yellow, with green leaves, and the symbols include bunches of fruit, a house—more like a castle actually—and four wands.

It Appears to be an Optimistic Reading

So what do I get from this little reading? Well, it looks to be an optimistic interpretation, although at the outset there seems to be a stubborn authority figure holding things back for the moment, and those mountains suggest there are major barriers to be climbed before the end of this phase of my life.

Nevertheless, another persistent person suggests later agreement and harmony with continued development and progress.

However, the gray sky implies my vitality is currently in short supply, so maybe I should take a vitamin or two before continuing the battle. It's generally okay there, though: The green foliage continues to express expansion, while the sun opens up new beginnings.

And finally the *peak* position. Well, apart from needing a vitamin boost, the project is doing well, moving in the right direction (even though it's mulishly slow), and will reach some kind of agreement pretty soon—although I still have to connect with that authority figure before the deal is wrapped up. And even when that's done, I need to decide which of several projects I should tackle next.

Much Work to be Done

Does that make any sense to you? Probably it's hardly crystal-clear, but in the broad sense, it's unmistakable to me. The project is this book. As I lay this spread, the book is only two-thirds written, so there's still much work to be done, and the deadline is approaching. But at least this is definitely a worthwhile effort: The contract will be wrapped up soon, and I'll decide whether next I'm going to write a book about the Tarot cards, take a shot at a bit of romance writing, or re-hash an adventure novel which I've been plotting for years. Stay tuned!

A final thought about this reading: If you're experimenting with this mind work, it's probably best to lay the cards out only once—shuffling the cards again and trying to get the answer you want to hear will lead to confusion.

And that's it. Congratulations. Two things will have happened by now. Either you're ready to buy yourself a Tarot deck and an appropriate book to start using the arcane wisdom, or you've gotten bored with the whole Tarot system and you're already reading further along in the book. Either way, I now change my stance: The Tarot material has done it's work. It's drilled its way into your subconscious and your intuitive skills have been further sharpened.

To Sum Up This Chapter

Here you've checked your logic capacity, had fun with the double-nose test, discovered your Destiny Number, looked at some basic astrology, palmistry and biorhythms, used your imagination in the wooden block test, and finally looked fairly extensively at the Tarot cards in theory and practice—although I said earlier on that if the Tarot is still in your future for you that's okay. You're free to abandon these particular concepts and pick up my narrative later in the book. Either way, you now know some more about yourself and your contingency talents.

Next, in Chapter 8, you'll find more advice and suggestions to help you further along your destined path.

Step 7:

This is the final step in building your fortune, be it material, emotional, or spiritual. Know that now everything is yours for the taking.

Chapter 8

Tips and Wrinkles

Calamaties are of two kinds:
misfortune to ourselves and good fortune to others.
Abundance is not something you acquire,
it's something you tune into.

—Gteof Gray-Cobb

This chapter gives you a segment of information and guidelines that add details to your intuitive structure—because it is a structure, in the sense that you create it by yourself. And once the whole thing is working well, you can sit back and enjoy the ride. Scarcely a roller coaster (unless that's what you'd prefer), but more like a smooth glide from wherever you started to wherever you want to be.

Sounds wonderful, eh? And it is, yet some people may wonder if this is really as marvelous as I say. These days there are so many scams and frauds that sometimes you might wonder, for instance, whether to pick up the phone lest some smooth-talking person excitedly announces you've just won the grand prize ... although once you look further, it may cost you mega-bucks to actually receive your prize, or you may have to pay a service fee, or something like that, in order to get the prize into your hands ... if it ever actually arrives!

So be doubtful if you like. These days, that may often be a good idea. You've already read seven chapters about this program and sketched out what you can do and what spectacular results can arise when you try the exercises and suggestions in this book. Yet I'm pretty sure some of you will be asking, "Where's the catch?" And if that's you, this chapter is the one you should lean on.

A Toe in the Water

Instead of plunging full bore into this world of happenstance as many people will do, here's how you can put just a toe in the water to see if it's warm enough. Then you can try another toe, perhaps a whole foot as you murmur: "Okay so far."

You could call this the step-by-step method. It works well for anyone who's skeptical, yet ultimately the results are the same: Lucky breaks and coincidences fall out of the sky and you reap the benefits.

You'll need the first three or four chapters of *Twist Your Fate*. Then, once you've absorbed those words, you can skip to Chapter 8, this chapter. After you've accepted that text, you can readily read the rest of this book.

So, as I said earlier, if it fits your psychological set, do indeed start small. That way you can adopt the magic of chance one bit at a time. May take a bit longer to create, but that's fine—maybe that's the way such intuitions will work for you!

So how do you do this? Slowly, right? Anytime you feel like it, you can stop and retrace your steps to come back to firmer ground.

First, you'll have accepted the basic idea of *Twist Your Fate*, suggesting that it's possible to change your lifestyle for the better. Then, you'll have thought about how you'd like to change your life. You'll have considered how to move apparent obstacles in your way, and the principle thought of giving yourself the okay to advance.

A Careful Path

Unlikely there'll be a flutter of angel's wings or vast signs in the heavens. Told you this would be a careful and cautious path you're treading. Yes, the first thing you're going to do is to find personal proof that what you're doing with coincidental working is actually working. Nothing big, y'hear? But something unusual and acceptable to your mind and convictions.

So what would you like to have happen? As I said, no rumbles of thunder, no flaming signs in the sky. Just a small coincidence that will have you say to yourself, "That's interesting, but I guess it's just a lucky fluke."

Congratulations! You're exactly on the glide path to landing on the runway to touch down onto those precious desires you thought about in Chapter 2.

You're right, it might have been a lucky fluke. But when you're ready, try the technique again and see what happens. Surprise! It happened again. Interesting. Momentous? The jury is still out but it's definitely worthy of note. But still a fluke, for sure.

So do it again. And again. Keep at it until your fluke thoughts starts to dwindle. Each time you get the appropriate result, you'll start looking for it. Eventually—and when that is depends on a whole passel of your personal logic, your skepticism factor, and your attitudes and personality—you'll kind of get a feeling that this preprogrammed event that keeps happening is somehow connected with you. And you'll be right!

Luck Turns Things Your Way

Somewhere along the line you'll accept that what you're doing is bending luck to turn things your way. In other words, you're in control.

I agree that may be difficult to accept for some people. So the thing to do is to try the technique again. Far out, as they used to say long ago—it worked!

Keep at it. Notice those strokes of luck and coincidences. Finally, you'll have repeated the proof so many times you'll truly believe you're in charge of this small process.

Then, once that feeling of belief seeps through you, you can start going for bigger *Twist Your Fate* happenings. It just needs the first nudge, and then things keep happening quicker and quicker until you can gladly say at the end of one day "I've achieved my personal success." And whatever that success is, you've already set it up in the beginning of the synchronicity process.

Sure, I know I'm holding you back. *Fer heaven's sake*, what is this thing you're doing that I keep burbling about?

Ready? What I'm suggesting you do is to somehow create a thoroughly material thing. And what might that be, *pant, pant*?

What it might be would be a ten-dollar bill.

(*Aw shucks*, and similar disgusted noises.) Major anticlimax! Were you perhaps expecting Cinderella, glass slipper, and handsome prince or princess to boot?

No Need to Stop There

Hey, it's small-step by small-step, remember? And producing a few bucks is almost certain to be okay for most people. The money will be real. You can spend it, save it, even frame it and keep it, if you wish, as the first of many ten-dollar bills you're going to create.

But, as I'll suggest again later, there's no need to stop there. Yes, you can make a ten-dollar bill this way, but you'll probably find it easier and quicker to make ten bucks by some other method, like mowing your neighbor's lawn or doing some other simple task that brings in money. There's more than one way of cooking an egg: Using *Twist Your Fate* is only one of many ways of producing a minor amount of money. By all means, as you experiment, use these methods to bring money to you, but be sure that this will be only *part* of the process—believe you me, we're only dipping into about half of the subject—the best is yet to come!

Now, how actually do you take control of these joyful phenomena? Well, considering the kind of stuff we're doing, there are several ways you can go. Your destiny, your luck, and your chances, you may have realized already, is only one of many different ways of getting results.

A Splinter of Motivational Knowledge

I've mentioned several authors in the introduction of this book, authors who have shown you how to create a new life for yourself. The portion of the method used here is merely a kind of leaf off the whole tree of motivational knowledge. This particular technique I'm about to offer you is tied into the theory of synchronicity which I referred to briefly in my introduction of this book.

Whether it's explained by the earlier heavyweight dictionary definition, or whether it's referred to as the two-word phrase, *meaningful coincidence*, synchronicity is still a challenging concept. The theory was created by Swiss psychologist and psychiatrist Carl Gustav Jung, and the practice of *using* synchronicity is one way of proving the *reality* of synchronicity.

And although Jung's definitions and theories are intriguing, what say we move on to practical usage of his conjectures? Here's the meat and potatoes of the step-by-step procedure built especially for the wary, the doubtful, and the skeptical.

Right Down to Your Toenails

Ready or reluctant, hesitant or raring to go, we're about to move out with new hopes, new horizons, and new values!

What you're about to do is to convince yourself right down to your toenails that you can personally control your situation, whatever it may be. By setting up relatively simple manipulations of coincidences, which you may call your fate or your destiny, you can bring small benefits. But never just one time—you'll find you can do it anytime, with a repeatability that first becomes surprising, then remarkable, and finally fabulous.

It's a case of discovering that when you've done it enough times to convince yourself you're controlling the process, you can then go on to bigger and better demonstrations of your power.

What you call the process is really irrelevant. It's the results which count whether you call them an application of positive thinking, affirmations, motivational mentalism, lucky breaks or anything else you prefer to name it. Whatever, it is comes from within you, and getting the process going merely takes a modicum of mental energy.

A Walk in the Park

Just as we explored in earlier chapters, first you learn to relax, then you will invite your Inner Mind to cooperate. Now, provided you're a die-hard skeptic, here comes the major step. If you're a believer of course, this step is a walk in the park.

No matter what sort of a visualizer you are, think—right now—about a small package you received. When? Your choice—yesterday, last month, years ago, anytime. But try to think about the package. And only the package—what was in it is unimportant right now. Size? One-hand size, maybe six inches long and an inch thick.

Now, with your eyes open or closed, your choice, pretend or visualize or think that you're holding that package we're thinking about. Now pretend the package is wrapped in gold foil, with a red ribbon attached. How're you doing? Getting the picture? Well, you're trying to, right?

Next, in your pretend thinking pattern, start to unwrap the foil. While you're doing it, use your senses. Feel the crinkle of the foil. Hear the small noises of the crinkling foil. See the changing shadows and lights as you turn the package over and continue to unwrap it.

A Material Reward

Remember you've done something very similar before when you worked on the visualizing exercise from Chapter 5, so this is only a kind of replay, but this time you get a material reward.

While you're pretending to unwrap the gold-foil package, think what's inside. The target is very simple and very material. Inside is a ten-dollar bill.

Hey, I primed your mind on that pages ago as I mentioned the ten-dollar bill and then moved on to another subject. So now it's literally child's play to pretend you're about to receive this piece of paper money.

Take off the last piece of foil. See your ten-dollar bill before your very eyes. It's a crisp new bill. If you're unable to see it in your mind's eye, tell yourself about it, as if you've got your eyes closed and you're explaining to someone what the bill is.

Describe its color, its shape—feel the sharp corners of this square of paper. Flick the bill in your fingers and feel the roughness of the paper between your fingers. Smell the fresh ink, see the printing on the front of the bill. Turn it over and look at the back. Hear the rustle of the paper as you do that.

A Five-Sense Experience

Yes, to make this strictly a five-sense experience, you could taste the bill, but that's hardly mandatory. But you can taste it, if you wish—after all, it's very unlikely you'll find any germs on a mental impression.

Next, while you're still exploring your mental images and impressions, conjure up a neat sense of pleasure and anticipation.

Think, or say: "I'm ten dollars richer. That's nice. And I can do that anytime." Say it with firmness and significance. Say it again. And a third time.

Then go back to whatever you were doing before you started this exercise.

What you've now done in your mind is to place a ten-dollar bill firmly in your future. It will come to you by coincidence: this is synchronicity, remember? In the next forty-eight hours or so, you'll maybe get a call from someone.

"I owe you ten bucks, remember?" they'll tell you. "Should I mail it to you or drop by this evening?"

Or when you run your bank statement, you'll find the computer says you've got ten dollars more than you calculated. Check the figures, if you like, but when the bank assures you that their figure is right, you can safely spend the small windfall.

Do It Again

When these things happen initially, stay calm and relaxed. Do it again. And again. Until you're absolutely sure that you're creating the whole process.

That's what happens: due to blind chance, money will come into your possession whenever you try this pretending or visualizing routine.

Does it always work? Sure it does. Perhaps it may take a bit longer sometimes. And now and again, it's something other than a ten dollar bill—often even more electrifying.

My son, who knows all about this purposeful stuff, still recalls how he swung into the car park of his business one winter day, stepped out of the car, and found an unidentified fifty dollar bill stuck to his boot.

Mind you, some people can be a bit too hair-splitting when it comes to uncanny coincidence rewards. On file, I've got a letter from a person in California who complained, "I didn't get a ten-dollar bill. My stepson, a real cheapskate, did give me two five-spots out of the blue. He's never done that before. Does that count?"

I guess I should have been more specific. You'll get the wherewithal one way or another: usually in legal tender, but occasionally from some other source such as barter.

And, of course, a ten dollar bill is fine, but once you get the hang of it, you can manifest any sum you really need.

I was working with this manuscript and got an e-mail from a colleague. These are her own words: "I had to test the manifesting of the ten dollars. I had to! Anyway, I did as you said—the gold package and ribbon, etc. One day nothing. Two days nothing. Then, the afternoon of the second day I went home to search for my husband's birth certificate. We'd just moved a few months ago and I hadn't a clue where our important papers were. Had a busy day at work. Was tired. Did *not* feel like looking for that darn certificate. I must admit, I was less than a happy camper and was pulling files out and doing the equivalent of stamping my feet. There, in a file long forgotten, was currency for an editing job done for a lovely man in Australia about two years prior—he'd sent me fifty dollars in Australian money. I have no idea how much that is in American money, but I knew immediately it was money I'd forgotten about." Yes, it does work, some how in your destiny's path.

Another example? This one was a biggie. It all began because one of the family members needed a cold drink while she was waiting for some paint to be mixed. The paint store did not have a vending machine so she went next door to get a cold drink. While she was in the store, she figured nothing ventured, nothing gained, so she asked for two lottery scratch cards.

"Yeehaw!" she said "I won, I won! Look what I've got—one of my cards is for a cool $50,000."

Mind you it's fairly rare to get such a significant sum, but all you have to do is keep your eyes open. Eventually, you'll notice the funds appear by coincidence whenever you wish them to. Then accept your control. Continue receiving these bonuses until you can say—and then believe—"I'm doing this myself," instead of saying, as you had previously, "What a lot of interesting coincidences have been coming my way." When you've gained that kind of competence and confidence, you can safely up the ante.

Chapter 9 will give you suggestions for moving further into this brilliant future you've been creating.

Chapter 9

Suggestions

*Recognize that it scarcely matters
what the world does to you,
the challenge is to disregard what's going on.
Once you get that into your Inner Mind,
little can touch you.*

—Geof Gray-Cobb

If you happen to be one of those people who overlook the beginnings of chapters so you can get into the meat of the text, you should swing your eyes up to the axiom above and absorb the words. Could be it's one of the most dynamic factors in your solving the synchronicity riddle.

That above maxim will pull you through all kinds of quandaries if you can understand what I'm getting at. You've heard the old saying *sticks and stones may break my bones but words will never hurt me*? Sure you have, but has the thought stuck in your memory? If it has, you should use it anytime you're frustrated by this world.

It works like this. Consider someone in front of you, someone who's avoiding laying a hand on you or actually breathing on you, but who is ranting at you and making vulgar gestures that are obviously pointed at you. Eventually, unless you're a saint, you'll get irritated. If the scene continues further, you'll probably make some comment which will no doubt escalate, especially if your opponent makes gestures inviting you to rumble. Maybe your adversary implies you're a coward or suggests something repulsive about your mother. Finally, the pair of you could end up exchanging blows. That's when the words stop and the bones start getting bruised and broken.

Two Items Added

Now set up the same scenario from the top with two items added. First, you're wearing a completely soundproof pair of earplugs. And second, between you and the offensive individual is a sheet of plywood which prevents you being able to see your adversary.

Now run the action through again. You're patently unable to see or hear the person who, in the original scenario, was bugging you. Notice the situation's exactly the same, but now, no matter what kind of rude gesture is made at you or what invective is yelled at you, you'll respond to the body language and foul expressions with calmness and poise. So what's changed?

In the first set-up, you were ready to start World War III when your adversary finally got too offensive. Now, in the second state of affairs, you missed getting annoyed and aggravated. Why the change? Because you failed to react to the hostility which was going on behind that sheet of plywood. Whatever was happening there, if you were unable to see it, then you would fail to react to it.

A Splendid Boost

Now if you can somehow set things up in your mind so that you fail to notice negative stimuli, at worst you'll be a much more relaxed person. And at best, you'll get a splendid boost of a pattern of dynamic energy affecting your destiny path. Work on the non-reaction method and you'll be virtually fireproof, at least as far as negative energies are concerned.

That's a thought to be getting on with, so now, before you read any further through this chapter, here's a simple test which will show you how readily you have absorbed the information so far. Read this test through to the end—it's brief, going from instruction #1 through to instruction #7.

Guarantee you'll find it interesting and useful, and you may also find that it tells you something about yourself that earlier you may have overlooked.

No paper or pencil required for this. The very fact of *being* is sufficient for this test.

Ready to take a crack at the instructions?

1) Stand up and raise your left foot about two inches from the floor. Hold it there for about twenty seconds.

2) Lower your foot to the floor.

3) Holding this book in your left hand, place your right hand flat on the right side of your head, so that your palm covers your right ear. Listen to what is going on around you for about ten seconds.

4) Change hands, placing the book in your right hand and your left hand over your left ear. Listen to what's going on for about ten seconds.

5) Remove your hand from your ear.

6) Take four deep breaths, breathing in and out rather more deeply than you normally would.

7) Disregard instructions number 1 through 6.

You'll notice that, in the opening paragraph of this chapter, I instructed you to read the test from the beginning to the end before performing it. If, during the previous few minutes you placed your hand over an ear or lifted a foot from the ground or took several breaths, you have automatically informed yourself that you are either unable to obey instructions or you were just being inattentive for the moment.

Alternatively, you may have been in too much of a hurry to be moving right along.

If, however, you arrived at item seven without having performed any of the actions listed under one through six, you're to be congratulated, and you'll probably find that you'll proceed successfully through all of the exercises and methods described in this book.

Future Reference

Of course, if you failed the test, there's no need for you to despair, but do store the thought away for future reference. Each word in this book is here for a purpose. I've reduced the techniques to a bare minimum, consistent with success for the average person.

Nevertheless, you need to grasp a certain amount of theory so that you shall be aware of what's being accomplished. Most of the effects described are so ethereal they hardly register on your consciousness as you apply the techniques. The knowledge of what's taking place is sufficient; the data will operate at all levels of consciousness and help to reinforce your goal-seeking.

So here are a few thoughts about the human mind that are somewhat metaphysical. Even if you've got little interest in the more ethereal aspects of this exercise, be sure that your Inner Mind is taking notice. Some people can more easily explore the metaphysical concepts of the human mind and soul by considering it as being like an ordinary hen's egg.

At a deep level inside the egg, in other words within the yolk, exist your subconscious and superconscious minds. I know I'm over-simplifying, but for the purpose of this text when I use the words *superconscious Inner Mind* or *collective unconscious*, I intend to mean the same thing. I have a tendency to refer chiefly to the *Inner Mind* merely because to me it's a simpler and definitely shorter term.

These imaginary egg levels—your subconscious mind and Inner Mind—are surrounded by your conscious mind, representing the white of the egg—while surrounding the whole, if we continue this analogy, is the shell.

Certainly, the shell represents prejudices, beliefs, and doubts which shape your behavior patterns. You can see that anything which proceeds from the yolk of the egg must move through the white and then through the shell. To continue the simile, if the shell is thick enough, then that which proceeds from within will never reach the outer world.

A Two-Pronged Task

So you've got a two-pronged task ahead of you. First you need to remove the shell from the egg, and then make the white permeable to data arising from the yolk. Having painted that rather inscrutable picture, you can abandon the simile of the egg, and consider your conscious mind and your subconscious mind.

The easiest, although somewhat imprecise, process is to think of the conscious mind and the subconscious mind as existing at different levels of awareness.

You know that, within your subconscious mind, the commands that maintain the autonomic nervous system of your body are produced. Also at this level exists the power that influences your physical body, but this same power also influences any part of the universe which it inhabits. Time and distance are of no consequence to the deepest levels of your mind; it's only at shallower levels that the concept of time and measurement become valid and important to survival.

Psionic Energy

The power we're discussing here we can call psionic energy, and now we're deep into a metaphysical universe. Psionic energy exists in a space-time continuum which is different from the space-time which your conscious mind exists in. Therefore, only by accident or under unusual conditions can the psionic energy from within the deepest levels of your mind be measured on a physical instrument. Normally, psionic energy operates and produces tangible results without any transfer of detectable power, vibration, radiation, or other emanations.

While we are discussing these levels of mind, we might consider the various radiations of mind, body, and soul as being on a descending scale of numbers, perhaps for the sake of convenience, from 10 to 1. The psionic power that we're referring to would occupy position #10, and as we proceed toward the lower numbers, we are arriving at the gross electrical effects that exist within your mind and brain. Thus, the neural electricity that an EEG (electroencephalograph) machine can detect is given the position of #1. Immediately above that, position #2 represent other nerve and brain activities, such as the alpha, beta, delta, and theta waves which are also physically measurable with the right sensitive piece of electronic equipment.

Position #3 is still an electrical or electro-magnetic position, and is roughly speaking where we should slot in conscious thought.

Then as we proceed to #4 through #10 we can allocate various mental activities to those slots.

So having made this admittedly artificial gradation, you can realize that the lower the number, the stronger the energy will be. Therefore, any kind of activity at level #1 will effectively mask, eclipse, and blanket any activity at levels from #2 and up.

So you can see that until your conscious mind can be stilled or harmonized (that's at level #3) with any activity occurring from levels #4 and up inhibited. This is why a fair portion of this book is taken up with techniques and methods for stilling the mind, of turning off muscular electrical pulses, of restraining neural activity, of reducing the alpha and beta activity of your brain to the slowest possible frequency. Then, and only then, is there a reasonable expectation for psionic activity to become manifest for you on a regular basis.

Lucky Breaks Possible

Once that energy is mastered, literal lucky breaks are truly possible: In fact, they're routine. The manipulation of apparently material objects is only one manifestation of psionic power directed by a co-operative conscious mind. Directed without obstruction, psionic power is the greatest force, the greatest energy that can be found in the space-time continuum that you're occupying at this time.

Back in Chapter 6, we briefly discussed precognition, the ability to know the future. That's certainly a metaphysical concept, the idea of being able to see the future before it's happened. It also creates interesting paradoxes and philosophical considerations. Assuming we can look up the time line and know that some particular event is going to happen in the future, is that happening predetermined so that it's going to happen whatever occurs? Or if the event you see happens to be something you dislike, can you duck it and avoid it? That's an interesting byway to explore, but we'll bypass that fascinating ability for now, otherwise we'll be into even deeper metaphysical water.

Precognition

The ability to know the future is called precognition, and many people have been able to look ahead, seeing future happenings, and even more amazing , they've told people about them, even written about them, well before the event. Sadly, probably because most people think precognition is well into the spooky realm of crystal balls and broomsticks, even when a seer gets it right and announces something in the newspaper before the event, very rarely does anybody take any notice.

So, although you can by now easily tweak up your intuitive facility and start seeing the future, my suggestion to you is that you keep it to yourself. By all means capitalize on your precognition, but unless you want to be labeled a kook and a nine-day wonder, going public about your abilities is unwise. About two thousand years ago there was a crucifixion, and although that sort of stuff rarely happens in this modern world, there are similar executions happening right in your own backyard every day, although nowadays they call them character assassinations.

So how do you foresee the future? Well, most of it you've done already as you've read this book. All it takes is a slightly different way of thinking.

Becoming A Future Reader

Up front, forget the idea of seeing visions in major detail with a calendar set up so that you see the coming event, allowing you to time it just right. Sure, you can do that, but maybe tomorrow or even next week: Like most metaphysical faculties, it may need a little work and practice. You've already got much of the start of becoming a future reader if you've tried some of the tests and techniques in the previous chapters here. That bit about self-hypnosis in Chapter 3 will help you a lot. Chapter 6, about relaxing, will also be useful. Training your visualizing ability, as expressed in Chapter 5, is another part of the preparation.

If you're determined to use your foreknowledge of events, here, briefly is how to go about it. There are many different ways to achieve precognition or prevision to become an oracle. Some of those methods are logical and others are strictly wacky. You can get involved in looking at tea-leaves or coffee grounds, reading tarot cards, noting the sticks of the I'Ching, and a whole host of seership stuff, including poking around a chicken's entrails. Unless you're really determined to try any or all of those things, you could try something simpler.

Buy yourself a sheet of white card, maybe about two feet square. Then paint a black circle about two inches across in the center of the card.

Pin your card against a wall so that when you sit down your face is about three feet from the card and you're looking directly at the black circle.

Half an Hour of Practice

Then, find half an hour for practice maybe two or three times a week. At the end of each session you should scribble a few notes about what went on. It's your journal so you should be straightforward about your sessions. If nothing happened, say so. If something did happen, if you saw anything, however unusual, note that down also. All you have to do now is to be ready to look forward to any results that may be realized.

Turn up the part of Chapter 7 in this book where I refer to what phase the moon was in when you were born: when things happen during your precognition sessions, it's most likely to come about when the moon's in that stage. Keeping your journal, you'll note when things go swimmingly and, often about fourteen days later, you may find your prevision abilities temporarily out to lunch.

Also check the barometer or the weather channel on your TV: When air pressure is rising, you'll usually find things easier in the precognition department.

Anything else for your prevision sessions? A small amount only: It's probably better to eat lightly beforehand—the pizza can come later.

Mentioning food recalls a very clairvoyant and psychic student from Montreal, Canada. Unlike most people who try often desperately to get a smidgen of psychism working, Martin, the student, was so wide open to impressions that they bothered him, because he could never turn them off. The answer for him was to inhale a dozen muffins: That effectively suppressed his clairvoyance until he got hungry again. So a word to the wise: should you find that you're a natural clairvoyant, psychic, and prevision expert, and you find you have trouble *turning it off,* all you have to do is to emulate my old friend, Martin the Muffin Man. Yes, sure—that's what his fellow students called him!

Loosen Your Belt

I suppose another item to check when you're starting a prevision session is that you feel comfy, loosening your belt and any other clothes that restrict easy motion. And I guess being in a draught-free environment around 70 degree Fahrenheit (about 22 degrees Celsius) would help.

Of course, what I've been mentioning so far in your precognitive path is your outer conditions: Really and truly, it's your inner self that's more important. Applying the relaxation as suggested in Chapter 6 is pretty vital to your success.

So you're relaxed and looking at your card with the black circle on it. As you sit there breathing easily and slowly listen to your body, think about each part of you, head, shoulders, arms, wrists, chest, back, buttocks, legs, knees, ankles, and feet. Recognize the feelings that are moving around you, and realize you're carving different neural channels, ones that perhaps have been dormant for many a long year.

Little to Write Home About

What next? Keep at it! Your first few sessions may bring little to literally write home about. But what's that? Has your world gone dim, temporarily? Maybe it was the electricity company changing generators. Or perhaps it was something else.

And what's next? Smog, yet? Strange but true—certainly you see something like a heavy mist drifting in front of your eyes. But stay cool—there's more to come.

See that? A flying saucer, perhaps? Certainly a flash of light, then another. And another. And did you see that bit of color suddenly turn briefly into a landscape or a bridge?

And now a face forms for a moment. The fog drifts away and things keep flickering on and off.

You're on your way to precognition. Keep striving: You'll be looking forward to your regular sessions soon as the pictures clear. The images you're conjuring up in the deeps of your Inner Mind can have meaning. Remember your journal—you may need it next time when more communication turns up.

One Special Day

At this stage, some of it will be useful. The rest of it will be interesting but may be somewhat lacking in coherence. You'll see people, animals, towns, storms at sea, calm lakes. And then one special day, your Inner Mind will stop sending you only tidbits of information. Instead, you'll get a distinct message, although it may be a mite jumbled. Right now would be a good time to crank up your dream journal from Chapter 3 and recall your personal symbols.

Partly with the stuff you'll get from your prevision sessions, augmented by your dream journal, you can build up a narrative. Continue with these metaphysical aerobics and you're home and dry.

As I promised you, you have precognition. Well done!

Just one other thing before we leave this section. How do you stop these visions? No sweat. You tell yourself the session is over, pretend that a curtain has been drawn across the scene, you put the lights on bright, write up your prevision journal, then get back to what other important thing you are scheduled to do next. Simple as that. And if you should find that your previsions start happening at inappropriate times, do what Martin did. Have a muffin! (P. S. It works for doughnuts, too!)

Did Your Inner Mind Pay Attention?

That was cool, but now that you've gone through all that metaphysical grunting and shoving, here's another thought: You've talked to Inner Mind a lot but are you sure Inner Mind paid any attention? Here's how you can get physical responses from your Inner Mind, and in that way, get answers from areas of your mind and brain that will startle you.

Got a minute or so? It'll take a little while to get this thing going, but I guarantee it'll be well worth it.

First thing is to do the relaxation from Chapter 6 until you reach the words, "Then put your feet on the floor again."

Stay where you are, relaxed and peaceful, then open your eyes, and put your hands where you can see them. Maybe on your chest, perhaps on your thighs. Your Inner Mind is waiting to see what's going on. So give it something to do: You're going to connect yourself tangibly with your Inner Mind. What you need is a signal so that your Inner Mind can answer any of your questions you may pose in your conscious, or waking, state. What you get is a simple *Yes* or *No* response, which may seem picayune, but when you become good at it, you'll be able to get valid messages from deep in your mind and soul, giving you answers you've never even thought about.

Talking to Yourself

You do it like this: Look down at your hands. Continue to stay relaxed and just let this happen. Either in your head or quietly out loud, start talking to yourself. Sure, we've done this before, so it sounds less freaky than it may have earlier.

What you should do is talk to your Inner Mind saying: "Inner Mind, as a vital part of this exercise, please allow a finger or thumb on one hand to move. That movement, whatever it is, will be identified as *yes* or *affirmative*. Please allow the finger or thumb to move now. Do you understand and agree?"

Repeat that sentence twice more.

As you're reciting this triple statement watch your hands carefully. Initially the movement may be slight. Personally the first time I got any response all I noticed was a kind of uncertain tremble of my right third finger. I know some people get a more definite reaction, ranging from something more than the simple twitch such as I had through to a definite elevation of a thumb. But whatever contact you get, make a note of it.

Next, having got your affirmative signal, state three times, "Thank you, Inner Mind: Now please allow a different finger or thumb to move. Movement of this digit will mean *No* or *Negative*."

Again watch for a twitch of your finger or thumb and remember it.

Can Be Tedious

So now you have a *Yes* and a *No* signal working between your conscious mind and your Inner Mind. Now you can start using it, although I agree that this method, while very valuable, can be a mite tedious. And I must warn you that your Inner Mind has its own priorities, some of them off the wall at times. Inner Mind even has an offbeat sense of humor, so when you're using this Inner Mind oracle be very specific in your statements.

Of course, even before you start solving the mysteries of the universe with your *yes-and-no* diviner, it would be a good idea to check out its accuracy, so you know you're getting the right scoops.

Start with simple questions, as unambiguous as possible. "Is my name Henry the Eighth?" should produce a definite *No* twitch, unless you happen to be the eighth husband of a widow who had seven previous husbands all named Henry. Ludicrous? Sure, but also in your Inner Mind's reckoning, definitely a possibility.

So try another question: "Is today, Saturday, July sixth, 20--? Again you should get a negative response (unless it really is that date).

Now ask a question that definitely has a *Yes* answer, like "At this moment, am I reading a book?" And once you've got this thing going well, you're off to the races, although doing it painfully slowly. And by the way, be careful with illogical or trick questions. Your Inner Mind will cooperate like mad, but it usually dislikes being made a fool of. If you ask, "Is my Inner Mind telling the truth?" your fingers and hands will probably just lie there inert.

Thank Your Inner Mind

And before I forget, remember always to thank your Inner Mind when it's been cooperative and you end a session with it.

With practice you'll get some amazing responses. Your Inner Mind is much closer in touch with your past, present, and future than your logical conscious mind is.

A person I know uses his Inner Mind responses to check whether particular foods are good to eat. Yes, he's a health nut and he likes to know whether a particular product has chemicals in it that fail to meet his criteria. He swears by the method, assuring anybody who'll listen that he has avoided all manner of nasty contaminants in recent years.

Closer to home, you can consider my partner: This last fruit season, she picked some beautiful cherries from the tree in our yard. She asked her Inner Mind seer whether the fruit was okay. Inner Mind gave a decided *No* and repeated it when my partner asked again in a different way in case she'd misheard.

That set her back on her heels. She was just about to make a cherry pie, but when she looked closer, as she was washing the fruit, she realized a small worm was wriggling around, peering at her with it's beady eyes. Then she realized there were more worms on the fruit: Closer inspection showed most of the cherries were infested with little creepy-crawlies. That sure saved us getting extra protein in our pie, and it also saved a bunch of innocent worms from being baked and eaten. Must be something in that karma aspect—but once again, I'm ahead of myself: The section about karma comes in the next chapter, although no doubt you've got your own ideas about it already.

Health Matters

To continue with the Inner Mind saga, you've established your *Yes* and *No* responses as I explained earlier, and now it's time to get answers. You can discover facts from deep in your mind about almost anything. One close-to-home set of answers may be to query the state of your health. Now, for such matters it can still be tiresome, but the results can be interesting and useful. A typical line of question and answer could be first to ask, "Is there any disease within me that requires treatment?" and repeat that statement twice.

If you get a *Yes*, ask, "Is this a physical malfunction?"

A further *Yes* might prompt you to ask, "Is the condition lower than my navel?" and so on, establishing where the condition is located.

Question: "Will this condition go into remission without special treatment?" Here you should definitely get a *Yes*, because all conditions will go into permanent remission for you in the next 100 years or so. Remember, Inner Mind is very literal.

For instance, assuming you've established that you have a an irritating rash on your buttocks, you might ask, "Will this condition improve if I use Vitamin X?" Inner Mind could well give you a *Yes* answer, even though the condition got worse: Inner Mind's thinking was that the condition did improve—it grew larger, so you now have the most improved rash in the city.

A Detective and A Lawyer

So to play the Inner Mind game you sometimes have to be something between a detective and a lawyer to get the specific and correct replies.

If you really want to extend this health area, you can diagnose yourself, bit by bit, using that system of elimination.

"Inner Mind, is my left small toe in good shape?" The mind boggles, but it can be effectively done. And when you discover what's wrong with you, you can establish how your body and mind will best respond to what treatment. Your Inner Mind can give you advance warning or reassurance regarding many health matters. But I say again, whatever you establish, be sure you also check with a medical person you trust.

Again, it takes a while and you need to evolve a system of elimination to get specific answers from your Inner Mind. But before we dig up really interesting stuff, let's get *down and dirty* and pose one question many folk will want answered: "What's the winning number in the lottery going to be next week?"

Now if it was entirely that easy, we'd all be plutocrats. Remember, there's only a certain amount in any particular lottery pot on each draw day. So if there's, say, two million bucks in the fund and then ten thousand people happen to get the numbers right that week, the dividend for each is only 200 dollars. Thus, if you're seriously going to do the Inner Mind game, you better hope that the week you try it, you're only competing with a few people instead of 9,999 others!

Apart from that possibility, you've a few more items to be figured out before you're ready to plunk down your cash. First you have to find out which lottery, and then which day the particular lottery's going to be run.

Assuming you've done your elimination trip you've got a lot more asking to go. For instance, if you're aiming to win the 6/49 you'll have to ask your Inner Mind three times: "Is the number going to be 49?" and if Inner Mind says *No* you'd go to the next number down. "Is the number going to be 48?" And so on for another forty-seven times three equals a hundred and forty-one twitches of your finger until you've marked down the necessary six numbers. Then, and only then, will you be able to dash off to the lottery booth and buy the ticket that may make you rich beyond the dreams of avarice. Dear Mom, is it worth it?

In another area altogether, you may recall I said in an earlier chapter that you can foresee the future. Yes, in a sense your Inner Mind can do that: But the challenge may be to get Inner Mind's data out in the open so you can read it. Some times no matter how much you call on Inner Mind, your fingers and thumbs will be totally unmoving. Why?

One reason might be that Inner Mind is indifferent to your questions—it's got bigger metaphysical fish to fry that you may never know about. Alternatively, Inner Mind may stay motionless because it would prefer to maintain the status quo that's existing at this time in your mind and body.

Shelled Out Ten Bucks

More than two decades ago I was experimenting with Inner Mind stuff, and I was convinced I could win a lottery by using the Inner Mind elimination system I've mentioned. Among the many lotteries I asked about, my Inner Mind revealed the Canadian Super Lotto One Million Dollar Lottery would be the one for me. So I invited Inner Mind to tell me when and where I should buy the ticket, asking at the same time if I would win a big prize. Inner Mind indicated *Yes*.

So I shelled out ten bucks for a single ticket and waited for the draw. It was to be on October 25, 1981, and my ticket number was 967484. I figured I was home and dry. Inner Mind had said okay, so I was disappointed when the million dollar winning number was 674151. The winning number was greatly different from my ticket number—I missed even getting a miserable $100 win for finding the last three numbers or even receiving a free ticket for matching the last two numbers.

Still Got the Results

I've still got the ticket and the newspaper clip of the results and it was many years later as I was experimenting again with the Canadian 6/49 lottery when I recognized my Inner Mind was maybe telling me something with those 1981 answers.

Notice those two numbers for the Super Lotto: 967484—my ticket—and 674151, the winning number. Now if you subtract those two numbers you get a peculiar solution.

9 6 7 4 8 4
6 7 4 1 5 1

Look, starting from right to left: 4 minus one equals 3. 8 minus 5 equals 3. 4 minus 1 equals 3. 7 minus 4 equals (you guessed it!) 3. And the last pair, 9 minus 6 also equals 3. Only one pair missed the boat: 6 minus seven equals minus one.

Something was nudging my destiny away back then—five threes out of six in a row had to mean something, surely?

In the end I figured it out, maybe only to some extent, but at least to my own satisfaction. If you turn back to Chapter 7, you'll find a section about *Your Destiny Number* and in the paragraph about the number three, it refers to someone being a writer and ends "will bring you recognition and wealth."

So my view about the early Inner Mind experiment, when all those three's came up, was that somewhere there was a hidden message which suggested *forget lotteries, you'll do better by being a writer.* And that was very true—I've made more wealth from writing than I ever have trying to win lotteries.

Very Close One Time

But to be fair to Inner Mind, I came very close one time. Still looking for the quick fortune, I asked Inner Mind where I should take another lottery chance. This time the British Columbia, Canada, Lotto 6/49 seemed to be the right focus and rather than go through the mind-numbing process of asking Inner Mind which of the 49 numbers would match to the winning six numbers, I asked Inner Mind what sort of a bet should I try. Elimination again, and the final answer was five one-dollar chances on a Quick Pick. It came close! On December 12, 1987, the winning numbers were 2, 9, 11, 31, 37, and 40 with the extra number 41. Four of my tries went nowhere but the other shot was 2, 8, 11, 37, 40, and 41. Only a small coconut, but I won $71.10 matching the 2, 11, 37, and 40. And the great-if-only was that if that 8 on my ticket had been a 9 I'd have raked in $168,331.00.

I still check in with Inner Mind regularly, but I realize that sometimes there are easier ways of getting something done rather than have Inner Mind give the answers.

And the party's almost over, my friend. But wait before you snap the book shut: Chapter 10's just over the page and that will finally wrap up this narrative.

Chapter 10

Afterthoughts

Life is a joke that's just begun.

— Sir William S. Gilbert
The Mikado

This concluding chapter describes developments of various techniques you've been reading about and, hopefully, acting upon. For instance, from Chapter 3, where you learn to see your Auric Sheath, one of the simpler extensions of your metaphysical expertise can be to be able to see your aura.

Exactly what your aura looks like varies, depending on whom you talk to. The basic assumption is that your aura is an energy field that extends up to about three feet all around you. Many psychics will *read* your aura, telling you about the different colors that exist around your body and what the different colors mean. You can even buy a machine called an Aurastar 2000 that uses biofeedback data to analyze your aura and make a photograph of it.

Seeing Your Aura

Using your own body, you can develop your aura-seeing talents relatively easily until, instead of seeing your Auric Sheath, you can also see your aura. Developing that phenomenon will increase your ability to astral travel and will also amplify your clairvoyance in a variety of ways.

To show evidence of your aura and enable you to see it, the brief instruction on seeing your Auric Sheath can be expanded to perhaps thirty minutes of gazing.

First, you'll need to rearrange the lighting. Second, you'll need to locate a mirror in front of you so that you can see the reflection of your head. Ideally, it would be nice if you could stand nude in front of a full-length mirror during your aura-seeing practice. If that's impractical, a smaller mirror will do. And stripping yourself naked might be advantageous so far as the exercise is concerned, but that's really up to you and your mirror—if you like the view, that's fine.

The average bathroom often works extremely well for aura practice because, usually, there's at least one mirror you can sit in front of, and you can usually drape the window, so the room is virtually dark. Added to that, a single lighted candle, put in a saucer inside the bottom of the bath, shades the light rather well and makes just the right amount of dimness. Just be careful with melting wax when you're setting this up. If the bath-and-candle method is out of the question, you'll need to experiment with drapes and lights until the illumination level works for you.

Once you're sitting or standing with your head or body reflected in the mirror, you're all set to start your aura-seeing. This time, instead of looking at your hands as you did during the Auric Sheath exercise, you'll need to relax your body and your eyes so that your vision begins to blur gently.

Look at the reflection of your head. Soon you'll see your Auric Sheath around your head. It can look like a two-inch smoky skin all around you. If you're practicing nude, look down your body and you'll notice your Auric Sheath is broadest across your hips and thighs, tapering down to a slim band of blue-gray beside your legs and feet.

Keep on watching this personal energy show, and you'll begin to see your true aura. It's a broad band of energy spreading eight inches or more from your body. Once you've got the knack of seeing the aura, just like seeing your Auric Sheath, you should look through the aura, rather than at it. While you're looking at your reflected head, take a couple of deep breaths. You'll find your Auric Sheath and your aura will expand temporarily.

Where you go from there depends on your metaphysical aptitudes: Some individuals get so talented at aura-seeing, they can describe brilliant colors that glow around the body. Other people intuitively recognize a person's health by looking at the aura. It's a case of different strokes for different folks, but it's clear that learning to see your aura helps your spiritual powers develop.

Reincarnation

So having found metaphysical bond with your body and mind, you'll inevitably start thinking about other enigmas. When we start to push the envelope of this material world, a frequent speculation comes up. Have we lived before in some other incarnation?

Want to explore that surmise? There are recognized exercises to examine your ideas on the subject, and some folk reach startling conclusions.

Some other narrative than mine can repeat the often hoary stories about people who have allegedly lived other lives. What I suggest is you find your own answers when you attempt this exercise; at the very least it'll be a fascinating mental work out.

If you're going to take yet another journey of the mind into the unknown, one thing I would recommend is that you include a sort of mantra to be used by yourself when you end any kind of attempted reincarnation encounter. At the end of the session count slowly from 1 to 10 and then tell yourself: "I am fully awake, fully alert, well and rested and in touch with my own world of reality." And next, before you forget it, carry out something similar to your dream journal, writing a brief record of your feelings, memories, and anything that seems significant. If you get memories of being *someone else*, keep those records separate. You should compare them with any other details that come through at later sessions.

Ready to begin? So turn up Chapter 3 in this book and reacquaint yourself to the dreamy state of self-hypnosis. Once you're drifting nicely, think about what's going on in your brain. Then run a mental trip backwards in time. Recall your last birthday, and remember what you did, where you were. Once you've got that going well, start bringing up earlier and earlier memories. Think about the first memory you have as a child. It'll probably only be a momentary flash, but something *way back when* will tweak your memory.

Now that you've tagged that item in your recall, tell yourself in your mind, that you're going to make a major leap back in time, far further back than your childhood, far beyond your moment of birth.

If your Inner Mind responds to this kind of thing, actually make the announcement, in your head, saying: "I am moving back in time and I will recall everything that goes on." Stay relaxed and listen to your mind, noticing any mental pictures, visions, even apparent dreams.

While you're doing this, pay special attention to what you believe is around you. Is it a landscape, a room, a city, a whatever?

Then ask yourself, "Is anyone else near me?" Listen, mentally or clairvoyantly for any kind of response.

Now do your *let's pretend* game. Tell yourself you are reaching into your purse or pocket for a piece of personal identity. While you're mulling that around in your mind, make believe you're looking at the ID and remember any name, place, or country that comes into your mind. At this stage, you'll either be interested in going further with this procedure, or you'll have decided you have more stimulating fish to fry. If you do decide to carry on in your reincarnation research, your next mental effect will be for you to pretend you're walking along a corridor toward a door.

If you're going to pursue this line of study, you should do nothing more than that, except practice the mental corridor walk for ten minutes each day for a full week. Although this piece of business may seem somewhat trifling, it's actually vital to the success of the next stage in this work.

So stay with it, and about seven sessions later, you should, in your mind, be able to see every scratch on the door and every piece of lint on the carpet. In your imagination, you'll have looked at the whole corridor and now it's time for you to open the door.

But sorry to say it's a trifle more challenging than that: This hallway in your mind is due to open up to the vast sea of knowledge known as the Akashic Record or Cosmic Memory. So it's hardly surprising in this imaginary place for you to find a guardian outside the entrance door of the library. Luckily, a library card is unnecessary for using the records, but you will need a password, somewhat like punching up your secret code in the bank.

So, here for you is a bit more mental work: You need to set up your password and recall it for later. Your password is simple but unique.

First, name a title or salutation, such as *Ms., Sir, Count, Signor, Fraulein*—whatever you prefer. Second, indicate your favorite color. Third, and lastly, mention an animal you like. Put those three words in order and *voila!* there's your password. You can have quite a fun trip thinking about Sir Blue Lion, Miss Yellow Gorilla, Señor Red Killer Whale or any other title, color of the rainbow, and creature.

Decide which password you prefer, and as soon as you've thought the phrase, the guardian at the threshold will have recognized you and your aura. At once the guardian will step aside and the library door will swing open.

Step through the door and look around. Imagine you're in a great library, but leave the books alone for the moment. Merely spend ten minutes looking around the shelves, familiarizing yourself with the space, and absorbing the details of this huge locale.

You may need as long as two weeks of your daily ten-minute explorations to build up particulars of the library. See the books on the shelves. Explore and check each section of the room.

When—and only when—you're satisfied you know this place like the back of your mental hand and you've built a clear picture of it as completely as possible, you can pretend you're walking to the section that has a book on your lives—a sort of metaphysical biography. Because of your password and your soul energy, the book will be specifically for you.

What you have there is a portion of the Akashic Record, or Cosmic Memory. That's a kind of celestial warehouse that shows everything that has ever been thought or done. Those records arrive on the scene as pictures, so any reasonably skillful clairvoyant can see and interpret them. Both Madame Blavatsky and Rudolf Steiner maintained they found information on the history of the vanished lands of Atlantis and Lemuria in the Akashic Record.

No need for you to think you have to be a seer—just take the book off the shelf, find a lectern, open the book from the first page, and start reading about yourself. Look at the pictures.

In capsule form you'll discover your previous lives; who and what you were, what you did, why, to and with whom.

You can turn toward the back pages and find out who you're going to be next time. The possibilities are endless—but then, so is eternity! Know in your mind that this is valid, and also vitally important to the fundamental nature of your soul.

Enthralling though they may be, it's necessary that you keep your sessions to the requisite ten minutes a day. When you quit each session, take notes for comparison with new stuff you'll get from this same book that's always available to you and is never on hold.

Further Help

And having absorbed the ideas about the Akashic, to help you further increase your relaxation and Inner Mind influence, I suggest you record some special spoken paragraphs while you are listening to your favorite music.

Rather than simply read the following passage I suggest you find a time when you are comfortable and peaceful, then record these words using your own voice. You can then listen to the words and music whenever you require extra mental repose and to boost your meaningful chance influence.

Your Synchronicity Booster

"You are listening to music—the end result of cooperation and creativity. You hear the words here between, behind, within, upon the music. As the melody and notes wake up your sense of harmony, of beauty, of rhythm, so these words move into your Inner Mind with the melody, opening paths of reaction and memory.

"Think about the situation—the spreading network of incidents, chances, plans and projects that have brought these words to your mind and brain.

"Ideas, concepts, visualization are the seeds of our meeting in the pages of this book. Take a few minutes to think about yourself. What are your senses detecting? You hear a voice and the music: Perhaps you hear other sounds behind or with the music and voice. What do you see? Open your eyes if they're closed. Stay relaxed, without moving your head, and consider what is visible to you? Even if your world is dark at the moment, look at the shifts of impressions reaching your brain at this time.

"What do you taste and smell, as the air moves in and out of your lungs? What does your sense of touch detect? Think about the impressions reaching you from your skin surface—the various pressures and textures against your head, neck, shoulders, arms, hands, back, torso, buttocks, thighs, legs, and feet.

"And as you think about your physical feelings, your body, let each muscle and sinew relax. With every breath of air you take you relax deeper and deeper. And any sounds you hear will help you to relax deeper and deeper. Relax on the sounds around you, the music and the words.

"You have opened up to the messages of your senses, relaxing deeper and deeper. Pass your attention from the top of your head, slowly down to the soles of your feet seeking out areas that may be resisting relaxation. Ask your body to relax wherever you find a corner of stiffness.

"And when you're ready, bring your attention back to wherever you are right now. Feeling peaceful and relaxed. You're coming back now. Coming back slowly. Feel yourself lifting back to the reality of the room, or wherever you are at this time. Coming back now. Almost back now. Becoming awake and alert. And you're awake. Open your eyes. You're fully awake and alert, feeling serene, happy and relaxed. Look around you. Experience what's round about you at this time, then go on with whatever you were going to do next."

Play those recorded words at opportune times whenever you wish.

Karma

So the lengthy journey from the first page of this book to the last has almost ended. You're to be congratulated that you stayed the course, from the introduction that launched the idea that *Lady Luck* can be embraced and controlled, through to the closing pages where we explored precognition and lottery winning and there's some more to come!

Grateful thanks for your staying with me as you've perused, maybe been puzzled by, and no doubt challenged my opinions. This substantial effort by both of us—with you doing the reading and me the writing —has been on my personal back burner for years. Now, for better or worse, you see the results. My hope is that you will gain precision, advancement, and achievement in your life as you absorb my ideas.

The purpose of this book has been to offer you pointers to take you further along a path that moves you deeper and deeper into metaphysics, and closer and closer to spiritual energies that can change your life forever.

As you'll have surmised, my personal path rambles between agnostic and pantheist, so I'm hardly going to lay a sermon on you, especially a traditionally religious one. One thought to send you is:

> ## Listen Up!
> *Be careful what you pray for* should be your watchword as you explore the interesting byways I've been indicating.

Well, sure they were attention-grabbing —if they were uninteresting you'd have thrown this book down hours ago. Yes, there are unusual ideas within, but there's a chance that if you're a wide-eyed idealist you may see this book and its techniques as open-season for making the entire world blissful and triumphant.

If that's so, please suck back and reload for a moment.

Yes, yes, YES, fortuitous accidents will work felicitous events for your personal pleasure. But if you're thinking you'll *do good* for everybody or anybody else in the world, please, pretty please with sugar on, think again.

There's no way you can decide what's best for other folks. Who do you think you are, anyway? Yet you can decide what's best *for you*.

Listen to those last two words. *For you.* Forget anybody else. Healing Aunt Maud's headache without you saying a thing to her is never the name of this game. Neither is confidentially bringing Brother Bill out of bankruptcy a good notion. Getting Joe and Mary secretly back together again might seem to be a splendid idea: Believe you me, that's probably one of the worst ideas since Moses was a little boy.

Those thoughts may be delightful, but sober advice is to mind your own business until someone asks you for help. By all means discuss the situation with third parties and when Aunt Maud says, "I wish you would get rid of my migraines," you can gladly (but I suggest secretly) use the Midas touch of fate to alleviate Aunt Maud's misery.

This kind of thing needs great care. Manipulating other people's lives is a big fat NO-NO! You may think you're doing Brother Bill a big favor when actually you're compounding the problem. Brother Bill got himself into his personal mess by thinking about it. He can straighten out his affairs the same way—doing it for him can be dangerous because there's no way of knowing what other people really and truly want and need when it comes to the universal scheme of things.

Could be you're messing with that law of cosmic cause and effect known as karma, a Sanskrit word. The idea of karma varies from one religion to another, but the belief is pretty solid throughout: It's okay to do good deeds. Yet if the results of a good deed are negative, you can still get the downbeat effect and find yourself doing another stretch of reincarnation, which is what karma's all about.

Try this for size. Imagine a poor old lady, the next street to you, is paralyzed. Maybe she had a stroke or she's a paraplegic because of a car accident. She spends her time sitting in a wheelchair all day. Now what if you could magic up an energy that gives her a total remission overnight? That would be a true good deed, right? Surely, you'd reach nirvana earlier after doing that wonderful thing?

But what if that old lady has been hating her next door neighbor for years, because the neighbor can walk and run while she, the stroke victim, has been in her wheelchair for years. So the next day, she walks to the store on her miraculous renewed legs and she buys a nice new, sharp kitchen knife.

The mobile neighbor drops by to see if there's anything the stroke victim needs. The old lady uses her newly-acquired hands and arms to slip the nice new knife into her neighbor's third and fourth rib ... and?

Fast forward shows the poor old lady can now walk around, do anything, but she's now in jail for life. So you gave her the mobility to do the murder, remember? Then are you responsible for the snuffed-out life?

Perhaps you bring your personal magnetism to bear and try to put the affair back on track again. Well sure, you might raise the dead, bring the cooling corpse to life again, perhaps from inside a coffin as you miraculously tried to put things back again. More complications. Solomon might have trouble deciding.

So just stay out of deliberately interfering with the fate of other people, no matter how good-hearted your efforts may be. And while you're experimenting with all this good stuff, keep your wonders quietly at home, in secret.

I say that because apart from the karmic consequences of your work, no matter how well-intentioned, many people have conflicting ideas about metaphysical working. There are still folk who feel that doing psychic work is immoral, sinful, wicked, evil, and just completely false.

What can I say? Yes, there certainly are people who think that way. Sometimes these critics of metaphysics have battened on to a particular set of beliefs which they hold like a banner, allowing no other view to be offered. Often they are religious fundamentalists who have been programmed by their parents or their ministers to accept a very narrow view of this world.

I'm in awe of such simple and unwavering convictions and I'd never try to alter their judgments. Maybe I'm a heretic or just plain unorthodox: My view of the world suggests there are many faiths and many beliefs that are valid. And if anyone has an aversion to the ideas I've proposed here, I think Voltaire might have the penultimate remark: "I disapprove of what you say, but I will defend to the death your right to say it."

And the last word (I promise you) goes to Dave Pelzer, a royal guide to incentive, inspiration, and encouragement. In his book, *Help Yourself,* he writes: "It's all in your mind. ... that's where everything matters."

Think about that seriously and well.

Glossary of Terms

This glossary of terms is intended to clarify the substance of the text. With each word or phrase is a definition or explanation of what the term is intended to mean within the context of this book.

Arcana

Plural term (singular is arcanum) of inner secrets or mysteries. As in the Tarot cards which are known as the Major and Minor Arcana or secrets.

Astral body

Occult thinkers suggest that as well as having a soul or spirit plus a flesh-and-blood body, we also have an astral body, a faithful duplicate of our material body, but made of matter that exists at a higher frequency than material flesh and blood. Traditional procedures allow your physical body to remain behind while your astral body goes on journeys and travels anywhere you choose. The astral body is envisaged as existing in the astral plane (c.f.).

Astral plane

Also known as the Astral Light, the Astral Plane is a sea of unseen energy beyond the range of our normal five senses. Nevertheless we're all connected with the energies of the Astral Plane, and within it is the Cosmic Memory or the Akashic Record.

Astral projection

See Astral travel.

Astral travel

A journey of your awareness out of your physical body, taken at will in full conscious control. Your body lies as if you're sleeping. You—the thinking, remembering, feeling, and experiencing you—are somewhere else at the time.

Inner Mind

A simpler and shorter term for the words *superconscious* or *collective unconscious*.

Karma

The law of cosmic compensation for one's good and bad deeds.

OOBE—Out-of-Body Experience

See Astral travel.

Subconscious mind

The engine room of your ship of life.

Superconscious mind

An all-knowing and close to omnipotent part of your mind, deep below your subconscious. Sometimes known as the collective unconscious.

Bibliography

Anderson, Mary. Palmistry. New York. Weiser. 1973.
_____. *Secret Power of Numbers*. New York. Weiser. 1972.

Avery, Kevin Quinn. *The Numbers of Life*. New York. Doubleday. 1977.

Bagnall, Oscar. *The Origin and Properties of the Human Aura*. New York. University. 1970.

Ball, Pamela. *10,000 Dreams Interpreted.* Prospero. 1997.

Barber, Theodore Xenophon. *Hypnosis*. New York. Van Nostrand. 1969.

Battersby, H.F. Prevost. *Man Outside Himself.* New York. University. 1969.

Bennett, Colin. *Practical Time Travel*. New York. Weiser. 1971.

Birns, H.D. *Hypnosis*. New York. Award. 1968.

Braha, James. *How to be a Great Astrologer*. Florida. Hermitician. 1992.

Brennan, J.H. *Five Keys to Past Lives*. New York. Weiser. 1972.
_____. *Experimental Magic*. New York. Weiser. 1971.

Butler, W.E. *How to Develop Clairvoyance*. London. Aquarian. 1968.
_____. *How to Read the Aura*. New York. Weiser. 1971.

Cavendish, Richard (ed.) *Man, Myth & Magic*, vols. 1-24. New York. BPC. 1970.

Chase, Jo Anne. *You Can Change Your Life Through Psychic Power.* New York. Pocket Books. 1964.

Cheiro. *Language of the Hand.* New York. Arco. 1968.
_____. *Cheiro's Book of Numbers.* New York. Arco. 1963.

Cohen, Daniel. *Biorhythms in Your Life.* Greenwich. Fawcett. 1976.

Crookall, Robert. *Out-of-the-body Experiences.* New York. University. 1970.

Dhiravamsa, V.R. *The Way of Non-attachment.* New York. Schocken. 1977.

Dudley, Geoffrey A. *Dreams: Their Mysteries Revealed.* New York. Weiser. 1969.

Dunne, J.W. *An Experiment With Time.* London. Scientific. 1944.

Edmunds, Simeon. *Hypnosis: Key to Psychic Powers.* London. Aquarian. 1968.

Fortune, Dion. *Sane Occultism.* London. Aquarian. 1967.
_____. *Practical Occultism in Daily Life.* London. Aquarian. 1969.
_____. *Psychic Self-defence.* London. Aquarian. 1930.

Goodman, Morris C. *Modern Numerology.* New York. Fleet. 1945.

George, Llewellyn. *A to Z Horoscope Maker and Delineator.* St. Paul. Llewellyn. 1976.

Gibson, Walter B. and Litzka R. *The Psychic Sciences.* New York. Doubleday. 1966.

Gray-Cobb, Geof. *Amazing Secrets of New Avatar Power.* New York. Parker. 1978.
_____. *Astral Travel.* Canada. Highway. 1973.

_____. *Helping Yourself With Acupineology*. New York. Parker. 1980.

_____. *The Miracle of New Avatar power.* New York. Parker. 1974.

_____. *Secrets From Beyond the Pyramids.* New York. Parker. 1979.

Gribbin, John. *In Search of Schrödinger's Cat*. New York. Bantam. 1984.

Hopke, Robert H. *There are no Accidents*. New York. Riverhead Books. 1997.

Hunt, Douglas. *Exploring the Occult*. New York. Ballantine. 1964.

Jacobson, Edmund. *You Must Relax*. New York. McGraw-Hill. 1962.

Jensen, Eric. *The Little Book of Big Motivation*. New York. Ballantine. 1994.

Knight, Gareth. *Occult Exercises and Practices*. England. Helios. 1969.

Leek, Sybil. *Numerology*. Canada. Collier. 1969.

Lind, Frank. *How to Understand the Tarot*. London. Aquarian. 1969.

Lopez, Vincent. *Numerology*. New York. New American. 1969.

Lundsted, Betty. *Astrological Insights Into Personality*. San Diego. ACS. 1984.

Malak, Frater. *The Mystic Grimoire of Mighty Spells and Rituals*. New York. Parker. 1976.

Marcuse, F.L. *Hypnosis*. England. Penguin. 1968.

McHargue, Georgess. *Facts, Frauds and Phantasms*. Doubleday. 1972.

Monroe, Robert A. *Journeys Out of the Body*. New York. Doubleday. 1971.